SHOTS ACROSS THE WATER

To Kelly

PATRICK NASH

SHOTS ACROSS THE WATER

TALES OF A JOURNEY THROUGH AFRICA

First published in the UK in November 2024 by
Journey Books, an imprint of Bradt Travel Guides Ltd
31a High Street, Chesham, Buckinghamshire, HP5 1BW, England
www.bradtguides.com

Edited by Samantha Cook
Layout and typesetting by Ian Spick
Maps by David McCutcheon FBCart.S
Cover images © Shutterstock.com
Cover design by headdesign.co.uk
Production managed by Sue Cooper, Bradt & Jellyfish Print Solutions

ISBN: 9781784779818
British Library Cataloguing in Publication Data
A catalogue record for this book is available from the British Library
Digital conversion by www.dataworks.co.in
Printed in the UK by Jellyfish Print Solutions

To find out more about our Journey Books imprint,
visit www.bradtguides.com/journeybooks

Paper used for this product comes from sustainably managed forests, and
recycled and controlled sources.

ACKNOWLEDGEMENTS

Every time I have done something good in my life I have been fortunate to be surrounded by wonderful people. This was the same for this book, so thank you all so much.

My wife Amanda Stone encouraged me to write the book and helped me every step of the way – particularly when I got stuck.

I wrote most of this book at Urban Writers' Retreat in Devon, Gladstone's Library in Hawarden, Flintshire, and the Garsdale Retreat in Cumbria.

The book was produced by the great team at Bradt Guides. Thanks to Claire Strange, Anna Moores, Samantha Cook, Ian Spick and David McCutcheon.

My daughters Miriam Nash, Evie Nash and Treya Nash have enjoyed hearing some of my stories and encouraged me to write them down. And thanks to my parents Norman and Mary Nash, who were supportive of their 22-year-old son undertaking what to them must have seemed like a dangerous journey.

If a copy of this book ever makes it to Rob Evans, please get in touch.

Finally, I must thank all the people who helped me on my journey. I hope that I have suitably acknowledged them in the story. There were so many people who were kind, generous and helpful. I particularly want to thank Michael, the Regional Director of UNICEF in Bouar, Central African Republic. Without the support of Michael and his family during a time of sickness, I expect I would have become much more seriously ill – or worse.

ABOUT THE AUTHOR

After leaving school in 1975, Patrick Nash worked his passage on a cargo ship from Liverpool to Melbourne, Australia. Arriving with £50 in cash and a cousin who put him up, he spent the next nine months travelling around most of the country and working in factories in Melbourne and Sydney to finance his travels and the journey home.

After graduating with an economics degree in 1980 he set off on his own on a journey around North and Central Africa, walking and hitchhiking over 14,000 miles.

When he returned, after more than nine months, he became part of the team that set up one of the UK's largest vegetarian food wholesale co-operatives. He went on to lead on the development of an eco-village in the north of Scotland. In 1999, Patrick set up the largest workplace counselling service in the UK, Teacherline, along with charities and social enterprises that worked in education to promote healthy working environments.

In 2005, while setting up a contact centre enterprise, he decided to relocate to the Welsh Valleys, an area of high unemployment, in order to create jobs and growth opportunities. Connect Assist now employs more than 500 staff, providing 24/7 support to many thousands of people who face challenging circumstances including mental health issues, poverty and debt, asylum seeking and more.

His first book, telling the story of his career, *Creating Social Enterprise, My story and what I learned*, was published in 2023.

Shots over the Water is his second book.

CONTENTS

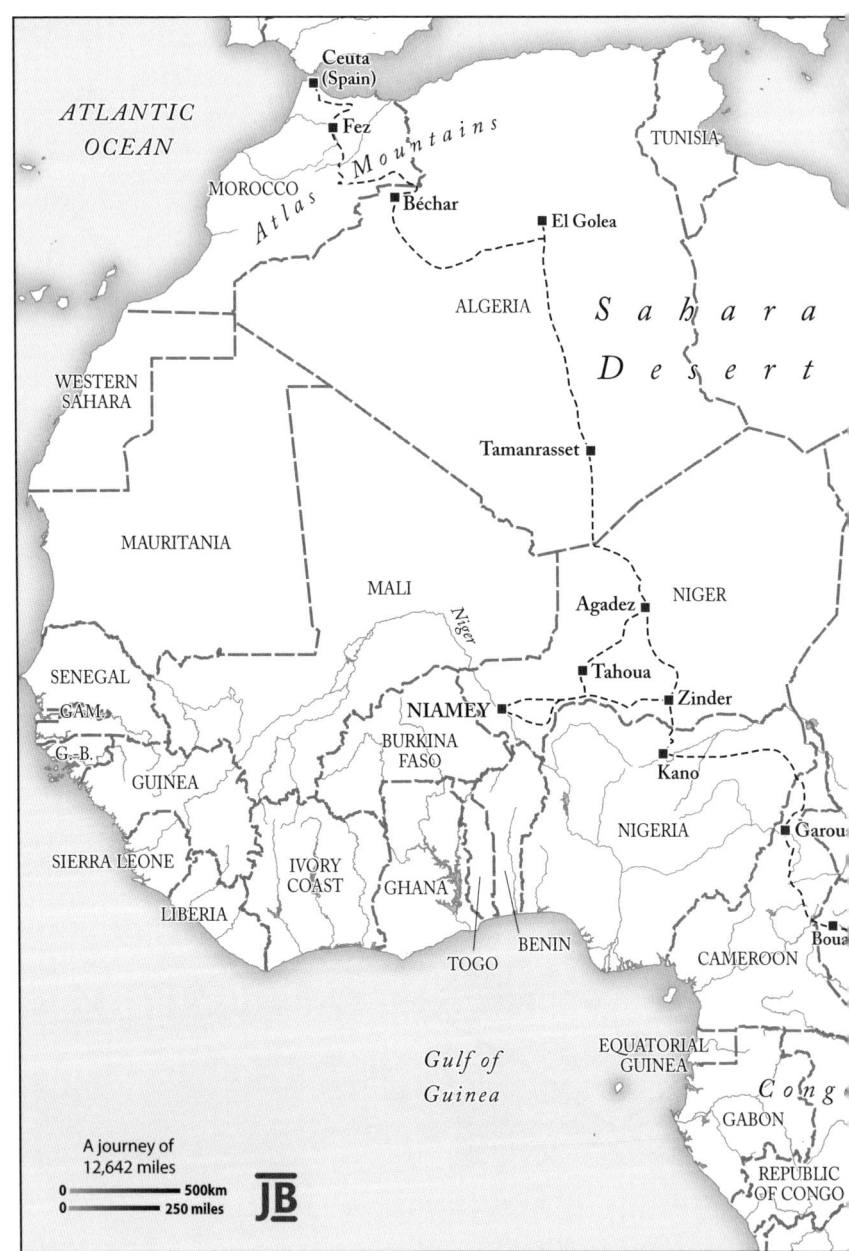

MEDITERRANEAN SEA

TURKEY

SYRIA

IRAN

LEB.

ISRAEL

IRAQ

Gaza City

KUW.

JORDAN

El Arish

CAIRO

1980 border between
Egypt & Israel

IBYA

LIBYA

EGYPT

Luxor

SAUDI
ARABIA

Aswan

Lake Aswan

Wadi Halfa

Red Sea

Nile

Atbara

CHAD

KHARTOUM

ERITREA

YEMEN

SUDAN

Blue Nile

South Sudan border
established in 2011

DJ.

ERITREA

Malakal

ETHIOPIA

White Nile

SOUTH
SUDAN

CENTRAL AFRICAN
REPUBLIC

JUBA

Gilo

BANGUI

SOMALIA

Gulu

Ubangi

Congo

Ituri

Lake Albert

GULU

Kisangani

UGANDA

KENYA

ainforest

Lake
Edward

KAMPALA

INDIAN

OCEAN

ZAIRE
(NOW DEMOCRATIC
REPUBLIC OF THE CONGO)

Goma

Lake Kivu

RW.

Lake
Victoria

NAIROBI

Lamu

BU.

TANZANIA

Mombasa

ix

PREFACE

It was our last day in Zaire and we were heading towards the border. We needed to get there soon, as our visas expired that day. As we got closer the forest started thinning out and we could see small grassy hillocks, fields and signs of agriculture. We eventually arrived at Zongo on the Ubangi River, the border between Zaire and Central African Republic. It was a tiny place, with a few shacks and a run-down immigration building with the roof falling in. It was quite chaotic. On the shore were a number of dugout canoes which were the only means of transportation across the river to the modern city of Bangui that we could see in the distance.

We were very relaxed going into immigration, our passports were fine and we got our exit stamps. The problem came when we reached the customs office, which was a tent on the shoreline. The customs official looked at our passports and then asked for our currency declaration forms. No problem, as we had got these signed at the bank in Goma where we had changed dollars into zaires, the currency. We handed the forms over.

'You have not spent enough,' he said. Rob, who spoke the best French, explained how we had travelled and that we had not spent very much money. This didn't work and the customs official became angry. He demanded that we pay a lot more, basically all the money we had. This sounded like a demand for a bribe. Luckily he had not taken our passports, which were back in our passport bags around our necks and under our shirts.

The customs tent was right by the dugout canoes and we had the exit stamps that we would need to enter CAR. The official went outside and walked to the immigration building. This could get very complicated. Rob said, 'Let's get in this dugout.'

There was one moored a few feet away and we ran in and told the ferryman to set off immediately. He got going at some speed. We were halfway across the river, which was fairly wide at that point, when we saw lots of activity on the Zairean side. Men were shouting and waving at us. Then a shot was fired.

We looked back and saw more shots hitting the water and only just missing our dugout canoe.

'*Plus vite, plus vite*!' Rob shouted at the ferryman.

INTRODUCTION

An intrepid traveller would now be hard-pressed to traverse the African continent at its widest point, passing from the Red Sea to near the Atlantic, while staying within a country that is not being torn apart by a civil war or recovering from one, has not suffered a military coup since 2021 or is not a failed state occupied by a toxic mix of rapacious politicians, militia and Russian mercenaries.

The traveller's undoubtedly inadvisable route would take them from the northern Ethiopian region of Tigray, at war until last year, then across Sudan, where an internal power struggle within a repressive regime has metastasised into general violence, and into the Central African Republic, now seen by many analysts as the best example on the continent of the worst that can befall a nation.

After this comes a difficult choice. A northern route could go via Chad, ruled by a 39-year-old soldier who seized power in 2021 when his father was killed in battle after three decades in power, and Mali, racked by multiple insurgencies, Islamic extremists and more Russian mercenaries hired by the second military ruler to take power in recent years. Another itinerary could take in Cameroon, convulsed by a lengthy civil war, and Burkina Faso, which suffered two military coups in 2022 alone.

Either way, our traveller would need – along with some very expensive insurance and much luck – the means to cross the keystone state of Niger, which has become the latest country to fall prey to what now appears to be endemic instability.

Extract from 'Niger's coup adds to chaos in the Sahel, but it may also offer some hope', Jason Burke, *The Guardian*, August 2023

In the spring of 1979 I was in my last year studying economics at Bristol University and finally knuckling down to revising for the final exams. Over a drink one night I was sitting with my friends Ann and Keith and the conversation drifted to what we planned to do once we had completed our degrees.

'We are going to Swaziland for a year with Voluntary Service Overseas,' said Ann[1]. 'We are really excited to be going, probably in November.'

'I'm thinking of doing a journey across Africa,' I found myself saying. I had been thinking about this, but it was currently only a vague idea rather than a serious plan.

'Where are you planning to go?' asked Keith.

'I'm not sure really,' I replied. 'Maybe I'll get to Egypt and just head south.'

'Well, if you keep going south you'll get to Swaziland, so why don't you come and stay with us when you get there?' Ann asked.

I know now that I've made most of the significant decisions of my life very quickly and often based on a chance conversation, a seemingly random thought or a moment of intuition. But in 1979 this was a new experience.

In January 1980 I set off on a journey that would define my life, crossing what are now some of the most dangerous regions in the world, especially as a young, naïve white man who lacked confidence. If you look at the Foreign Office travel advice today you would be clearly advised not to do this trip. All but one country I travelled through have significant areas showing *Advice against all travel* (shaded red) with much of the rest being *Advice against*

---

1   ⏳ vsointernational.org

all but essential travel (shaded yellow). If one of my daughters suggested they wanted to do this journey, I would do everything I could to dissuade them.

And yet I survived a trip that took in Gaza, Egypt, Sudan (including what is now South Sudan), Uganda, Kenya, Democratic Republic of Congo (then named Zaire), Central African Republic, Cameroon, Nigeria, Niger, Algeria and Morocco. There were moments that were dangerous, periods of illness, times when I felt despairing and many times when I thought I could not carry on.

WHY DID I GO?

When I left school in 1975 I was desperate to travel. Although shy and socially awkward, I built up some confidence travelling to Australia working my passage on a cargo ship, then working and travelling by coach around that large country. After nine months I returned home and went to university for three years. One summer I hitchhiked to Greece and slept rough on the beaches. I funded this by working 12-hour night shifts in pickled onion factories and camping in fields in the Netherlands. I once slept a night under a bush next to the Colosseum in Rome. I had some travel experience.

After three years at university I still had itchy feet. I finished my studies in 1979 but could not face the prospect of a career. Almost all the students around me were interviewing for banks, accountancy firms and the civil service. All were my idea of hell.

I had heard lots about the overland route to India and met a few people that had done it. It was appealing. Turkey, Iran, Afghanistan, Pakistan and India excited me as countries to visit. Then in early 1979 the Shah of Iran was overthrown and later that year the US

Embassy was seized along with 66 Americans, the majority of whom were held as hostages for over a year. A month later the Soviet Army invaded Afghanistan. Suddenly this wasn't such a feasible overland travel route.

The conversation with Ann and Keith turned a vague idea into a sort of plan. As I thought about it I soon realised that I knew very little about the continent. I had a rough idea of the geography, I had studied the history of ancient Egypt at school and I had read Conrad's *Heart of Darkness*. That was pretty much the sum total of my knowledge.

Most maps of the world have a size bias towards the north. I didn't think Africa looked that big! What a fool I was. The journey didn't look that far, but needless to say I underestimated how long it takes to travel hundreds of miles of dirt tracks balanced on the top of old lorries. Or walking all day in a hot, humid climate. Or crossing the sand track of the world's largest desert. I didn't think about any of this. I look back at my 22-year-old self and don't recognise how unprepared and frankly casual about this trip I was. To their considerable credit my parents were supportive.

PREPARATION

I turned 22 years old in October 1979. I was about five foot eight inches tall, skinny, with messy, scruffy blond hair and a beard and moustache. I wore thin round metal John Lennon glasses from the NHS. My skin turned brown easily and still does. I was a vegetarian and although I sometimes eat fish now, I don't eat meat, having a lifelong hatred of the taste and texture, how it makes me feel and the politics of food. I gave no prior thought to what I would be able to eat on this journey.

I didn't do much planning, but what little plan I had was first to fly to Israel and work as a volunteer on a kibbutz. I had developed an interest in communities and co-operatives while at university and this seemed like a great opportunity to experience this type of living before travelling to Egypt. The fact I could travel to Israel and enter Egypt from there was possible due to the Camp David Accords of 1978 followed by the Egypt-Israel peace treaty signed in 1979. As a result the normalisation of relations between Israel and Egypt would go into effect in January 1980, and the border between the two countries, in the middle of the Sinai Desert, would open.

I decided that I would need a second passport. Many of the countries that I would subsequently travel through would not let me enter if I had an Israeli stamp in my passport. I had no idea whether I would be able to get a second passport but in December 1979 I went to the Passport Office in Petty France, Westminster and waited in a queue for about an hour.

When I got to the desk I explained my situation.

The very helpful woman behind the desk said, 'We typically issue these for business travellers and require a letter from your employer.'

'I'm not a business traveller,' I replied, 'but a second passport would make a difference to my ambition to visit Israel and then travel across the new border to Egypt.'

She must have taken pity on me as she asked me to wait while she consulted with her superior. Another hour passed and eventually she returned with the manager. I was taken to a small room where I explained that I meant to travel from Israel to Egypt and from there south to Swaziland. They both took notes and then told me to leave my existing passport with them along with the two passport photos I had brought and come back the following week.

The following week the woman I had originally met presented me with my second passport along with my existing passport and wanted to know all about my travel plans. She was clearly interested and I think she may have swung a decision for them to agree to this. It is still possible to get a second UK passport but it's not something the government shouts about.

I spent December getting a variety of inoculations – against cholera, hepatitis B, rabies, meningitis, polio, tetanus and more. I got a year's supply of malaria tablets. I had the second gamma globulin shot (against hepatitis B) two days before Christmas and was ill for a week.

I bought a canvas rucksack about 13 inches square and 8 inches deep. It was small, but roomy enough for three light shirts, two pairs of light walking trousers, three pairs of socks and underpants and a light sweatshirt for the cold. I added a couple of books, a map of Africa, four small notebooks to write a diary, two pens, my year's supply of malaria tablets, some plasters, a small sewing kit and a mosquito net. Tied to the base of the rucksack was a small one-person tent and sleeping bag. I packed a collection of postcards of famous London sights, as I'd read somewhere that it was good to have a gift to give to people along the route. I didn't take a camera as I felt that this would create a distance between me and the people that I met along the way. I wore a wallet around my neck which held my passports and vaccination certificates and my trousers were held up by a money belt with a zip on the inside that contained £250 worth of carefully folded US dollars in cash, worth about £1,400 today. I hoped that would be enough.

In January 1980 I left my family home in south London. I didn't have a job or a partner to come back to. I didn't have a schedule or plan other than to fly to Israel, travel overland to Egypt and head south to Swaziland. I could have travelled on an organised tour in a lorry and with a group of people just like me. But I didn't want that. I wanted to travel the same way that local people travelled.

This journey set me up for the rest of my life and career. If I had not done it, I don't think I would have made the decisions that I subsequently made. I first got inspired by a business idea in the only backpacker hostel in Juba, South Sudan. This was a pivotal career moment, which of course I didn't realise at the time.

ABOUT THIS BOOK

The starting point for this book was a collection of handwritten diaries in small notebooks that I wrote on my journey. Because of this source material, much of the book reads in the voice of my 22-year-old self, although while drawing the text together I have been able to reflect somewhat. As I wrote, I remembered a lot more than was noted in my diaries, including some of the conversations that I had along the way.

For ease of reading almost all of the dialogue is in English, although much of it was spoken in French as well as some of the main trade languages[2] – Arabic, Swahili and Lingala. Temperatures are in degrees Celsius.

---

2   Trade languages, systematically used to make communication possible between groups of people who do not share a native language or dialect, were developed largely to facilitate trade. As I mostly travelled on trade routes, these were the languages I heard and attempted to learn a little of.

1

ISRAEL, GAZA AND EGYPT

ISRAEL

WARM WELCOME

On January 8th, 1980, I boarded an El Al flight from London to Tel Aviv. Passing through security took over an hour, unsurprisingly given the occasional hijacking of Israeli planes. I was more apprehensive about travelling than I'd felt before. It was some time since I'd travelled on my own and I was uncertain about the way things would turn out.

At the airport there was a crowd of people my age going to stay on a kibbutz who clearly had settlements to go to. I had not thought of organising this in advance and had absolutely no idea what I would do when I arrived. I sat next to a woman called Jaffa and we got talking. 'I'm going home to visit my family,' she said. 'They will be disappointed as I've just got engaged to my boyfriend and he can't take the time off work. Why are you going to Israel?'

'I want to spend time on a kibbutz,' I replied, 'and then I plan to cross the border to Egypt and travel down to Swaziland.' I made it sound so easy. We chatted for a while about my plans, such as they were. Eventually I decided to ask her what she knew about working on a kibbutz and in particular how I could get to volunteer for one.

'That could be difficult,' said Jaffa, proceeding to explain all about living on a kibbutz, which she had done a few years earlier. 'I suggest that you go to the kibbutz office in Tel Aviv where you can

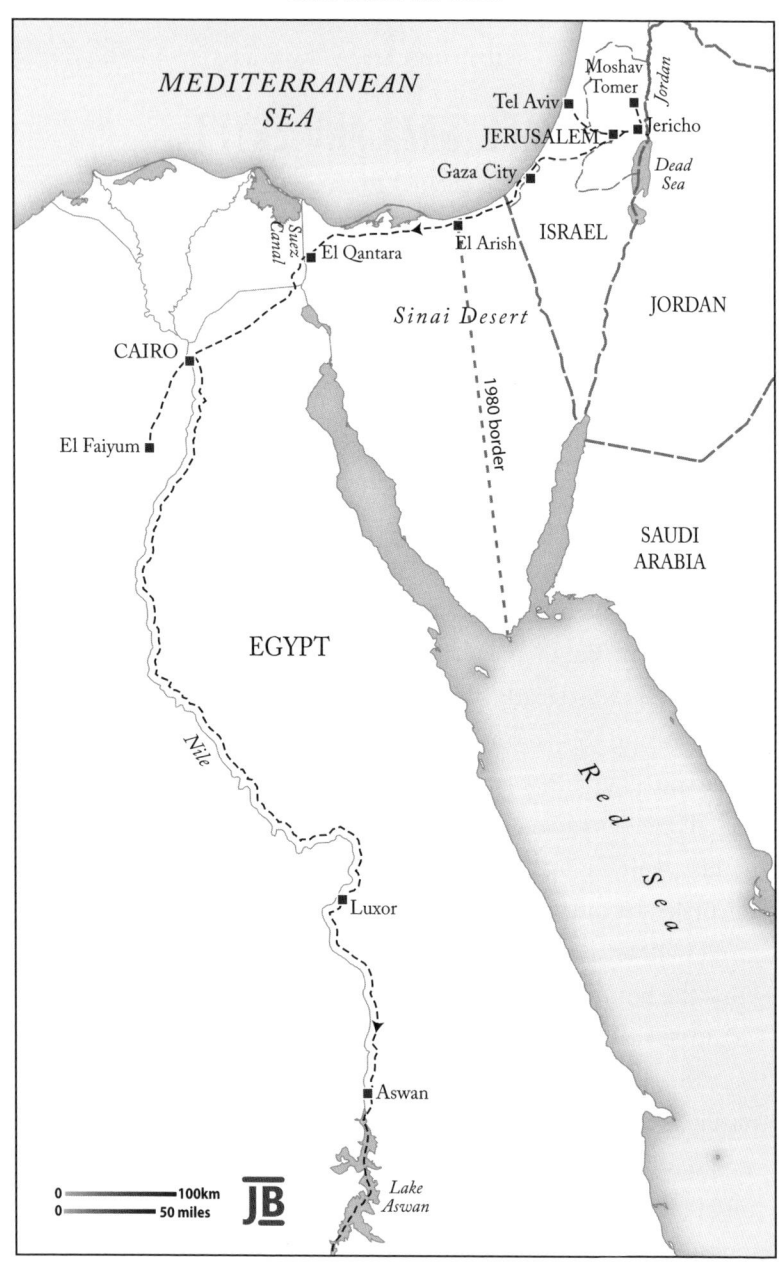

check on what's possible. However, many young people are doing this and most of them book before they leave.'

I felt a bit stupid for not having looked into this but there was nothing to be done. We chatted for much of the rest of the flight and as we approached Tel Aviv, Jaffa invited me back to her parents' house to stay the night. I was really surprised, although this set the tone for much of the rest of my journey. When we arrived the whole family were there to welcome her home. For some minutes they clearly thought I was her fiancé as they were all very welcoming, but even after Jaffa had clarified that I was just a man she'd sat next to on the plane, their exuberant welcome continued. Her parents insisted I should stay with them and that was that, as everyone piled into a minibus and headed north to Netanya, a 45-minute drive away.

There was an enormous tea when we got to their house, followed by a massive dinner later. Jaffa had six brothers and sisters and their flat was full of friends. The warmth and generosity of these people was new to me and I was plied with questions all evening by one person after another.

The next day I took the bus into Tel Aviv with Jaffa's brother Jamin. It was a big city with tall buildings, lots of noisy traffic and plenty of people on the streets, many of them in military uniforms. Walking down the streets facing west I could see views of the bright blue Mediterranean Sea. I loved the noise, the bustle and, most of all, the food.

'My favourite place to eat is the bus station,' said Jamin. We went to the square, surrounded by falafel stalls, where the buses arrived and departed. 'We will each buy a pitta bread filled with some falafels and then walk around tables with thirty to forty dips and salads, fill up the pitta with these, eat as much as possible without eating the pitta itself and then fill it up again.' There was every vegetable I had ever seen and more, all sorts of salads, olives, gherkins and other pickled vegetables and all sorts of dips including hummus, tahini, mint and yoghurt and much more. This was vegetarian food heaven.

Jamin was a few years older than me, living in a small studio near the bus station. He took me to the kibbutz office but, as his sister had suspected, there were no volunteer opportunities available. The person at the kibbutz office suggested we go to the moshav office. I had never heard of a moshav.

A moshav is a co-operative agricultural community of individual farms originally pioneered in the early 1900s. This sounded similar to a kibbutz. Jamin took me to the office, where they took my details, saying that they would look for an opportunity for me and that I should come back the following week. I spent the next two days with Jamin, staying in his apartment, where I slept on a large cushion on the floor. We had a great time as he showed me around the city and met lots of his friends.

Jamin insisted we travel to Kadima for the weekend, where the family had a country home. We were met by Jamin's brother, Gadi. That evening I joined their Sabbath meal wearing the *kippah*, the cap that covers the crown of the head and is worn for religious events.

On Saturday we went for a drive in Gadi's tractor.

'Have you ever shot a pistol?' he asked.

'No, I haven't.'

'You will today,' he replied.

We visited a wood where Gadi taught me how to shoot a pistol and I shot oranges on a tree stump, managing to hit a few of them. I was a bit shocked to be firing a weapon, although this is standard for all Israelis.

I still found it hard to believe that I had been so welcomed into this family all because of a chance conversation on a plane. It was the beginning of many such meetings with many families.

MOSHAV TOMER

I went back to the moshav office and sure enough they had a volunteer placement for me. Saying goodbye for now to Jamin, I took a bus to Jerusalem. It was a beautiful drive through the hills in a bus full of people all talking to one another. I got chatting to a group of women and men about my age who were doing military service and heading to a place south of Jerusalem which they obviously could not tell me the location of. It was fascinating to hear about their experience. Most Israeli citizens over the age of 18 had to serve in the Israel Defence Forces. There were many exemptions, although a lot of those exempt from military service did volunteer in any case. Men served for a minimum of 32 months and women for a minimum of 24. And all could be called up again at a moment's notice when required.

I changed buses in Jerusalem and headed eventually to Tomer, a moshav settlement on the West Bank close to the border with Jordan. Jerusalem is high up in the hills, 2,444 feet above sea level. The bus wound down steep roads eventually to Jericho, the lowest city on earth at 820 feet below sea level. The road was dusty and at points I looked out of the window and faced a huge drop close to the side of the bus as it snaked around hairpin bends down to the Jordan Valley.

The bus didn't stop inside Jericho, which was and is a Palestinian city, not open to Israelis. I would be able to visit it later. On this day I headed on to Tomer with the road heading north to the west of the River Jordan. About 40 minutes later I saw a small settlement of mostly white buildings located on a hill just above the road: my home for the next seven weeks. I climbed off the bus and walked up the hill to the moshav. When I arrived I was shown to the office, where I was assigned to a farmer named Michra. There was a house set aside for the foreign volunteers, of which there were three with a promise of more arriving soon.

The next morning I was awake at 5am and went to the house of Michra, 'my' farmer. He met me at the door with a beaming smile and, 'Welcome to Tomer, Patrick. Come in and have some coffee.' His English was good and once inside I met his wife and young son. Over coffee he explained that his crops were fruit and vegetables, grown on the land to the east of the road and going down most of the way to the Jordan River, the border with Jordan. We drove down to the fields on his tractor where my work entailed cutting vines and laying plastic over the watermelon seedbeds and later sowing courgettes, tomatoes and cucumbers.

Over the next seven weeks I worked in the fields, working the hard ground. We laid down irrigation pipes that dripped water (a technique I've used for growing vegetables ever since). We sowed seeds, weeded and soon after harvested as everything grew so fast. It was hard physical work and at times I wondered how I could carry on, surviving by drinking plenty of water and endlessly snacking on sunflower seeds.

The moshav had been established three years earlier and the farmers and their families were all quite young. I later learned that Israeli settlements in the West Bank are considered illegal under international law, although the Israeli Government disputes this. Being close to the Jordanian border there were regular incursions by the Palestinian Liberation Organisation (PLO). A few nights after I arrived a number of PLO soldiers crossed the river and there was a shoot-out between them and the Israeli army. Michra was called out at 3am and he took his machine gun into the fields for the next couple of days. We volunteers were ushered down to a bomb shelter underground.

This book is about my travels in Africa so I'm not dwelling on my time at Tomer. I worked in the fields six days a week. On my day off I would typically go to Jericho and a couple of times I went to Tel Aviv where I met up with Jamin. I enjoyed these visits a lot. In Jericho I would sit in cafés with the older men and play the Arabic version of backgammon called Shesh Besh. I began to learn some words of Arabic and had some basic conversations. One day we were sitting outside a café and there was a small snowfall. The men pointed at the snow and asked me what this was. This is the lowest city on earth and they had never seen snow before, not even having a word for it. It was my first experience of climate change.

In Jerusalem I began to learn the art of bargaining. It took me some time to get the hang of this as I felt so guilty bargaining with people much poorer than me. I soon discovered that the sellers were proud of the bargaining process, which was seen as a sign of respect.

I enjoyed the farmers I worked with, especially Michra. I enjoyed many of the settlement people and I had a good time with the volunteers. But I started to get itchy feet and wanted to start my travels in Africa. I did wonder why I had come first to Israel, but on reflection it was a period of adjustment after three years at university and I needed the structure that working on the land provided. After six weeks I felt ready to move into being a traveller and taking my chances on the road without always knowing what I would do each day, how and what I would eat and where I would sleep for the night.

I kept trying to find out information about when the Israeli/Egyptian border in the Sinai Desert would open to travellers. It wasn't easy to get but at the end of February I received news that it was opening in a week or two. I started making plans and told Michra that I would leave soon. He was very generous about this and he and his family invited me to dinner on my last evening. I gave them the first of my London postcards. I said my goodbyes to my other volunteer friends with promises to meet up again, which hasn't yet happened. I left Tomer in early March, taking the bus to Jerusalem, and stayed overnight.

GAZA

The next morning I tried to get transport to Gaza. I took a bus to Beersheba through beautiful hills covered with olive trees, although the view was marred by heavy rain.

At Beersheba I got a lift for most of the way to Gaza with a friendly Israeli postman. After I was dropped off, I waited at the side of the road for quite a while, hitchhiking in a large group of 14 Israelis with none of the ordered queuing I was used to in Britain. After staying with the Israeli group and seeing two other large groups of hitchers appear and disappear, with me still standing, I finally walked over to the Palestinian travellers on the other side of the road. Prior to coming here I had little understanding of Israel and Palestine and in particular the separation of peoples who shared the same land.

In terms of hitching, these Palestinian travellers had the situation far more under control. I asked one man standing there how to get to Gaza and he explained in a type of sign language that we should take a taxi that had just arrived. Within seconds a crowd had appeared and the taxi filled, costing very little each. My mute friend and I got in the taxi and we had a really fast conversation where he wrote on the back of the seat with his fingers and I spoke and wrote what I said. It was an extraordinary communication – he could not speak at all and I could not speak his language and yet somehow I learned about his life and told him about the trip I was now embarking on. He was a fascinating person and I learned then that one of the most important things while travelling is to find a way to communicate with whomever I am with.

Arriving in Gaza I said goodbye to my travelling companion and found an old and run-down hotel with a large, bare room with little furniture. It was very quiet and had a Victorian-colonial feel about it. There was a very nice old man working there who spoke a little English in a Scottish accent. He helped me plan the next day's trip – a bus to Rafah at 7am, then change money and get a taxi or hitch to North Sinai and the border. That was the extent of his knowledge.

January 27th, 1980 was supposed to have been the day that the borders between Egypt and Israel were opened to normal traffic on land and in the air, but the first tourists who tried the crossing were turned back by the Egyptians[3]. It took some time for the

---

3 ⬦ washingtonpost.com/archive/politics/1980/01/28/egypt-and-israel-open-border-but-traffic-is-curbed/84a7a919-d0e3-44dc-82a7-b511c2242aa8

situation on the ground to catch up with the new reality. As a result, it turned out that I was among the first backpackers on foot to make the crossing.

The next morning I took the bus from Gaza to Khan Yunis in the southwest of the Gaza Strip. From there I took a shared taxi to Rafah, much like the vehicle I had travelled in the day before. Then I got a bus to the border at El Arish, travelling through the desert on a rutted and bumpy sand road, arriving mid-morning. There I met Klaus, Henk and Rich, backpacker travellers like me hoping to cross this relatively new border. At the border it was a pretty simple process leaving Israel and I used my second passport to receive the exit stamp. I had expected to walk across the open distance but we were all forced to pay to get a bus across 'no man's land'. There was a large military presence: soldiers, guns and tanks.

EGYPT

YOUNG BORDER

On the Egyptian side there was a two-hour wait to enter and change money. We could only change up to five US dollars for each day our visa permitted us to stay in the country. I guessed correctly that this would be more than I would need. The bank manager was great fun and gave me a cigarette. We then waited in the police office where the policemen were excited to have Western travellers. The four of us sat on chairs and we were brought small glasses of Koshary, a delicious black tea brewed with cane sugar and fresh mint leaves. After a dusty wait outside the border buildings, this was really refreshing.

Then there was a flurry outside the door and in swept a large man in desert combat uniform, with a peaked hat and wearing a few medals.

'Welcome to Egypt,' he said very proudly. 'We are very pleased to have you visiting our country.' His English was very good, putting my very limited Arabic to shame.

I thanked him in Arabic and carried on in English. 'We are very honoured to be welcomed to your country.'

'The honour is ours,' he replied. 'I am the officer in charge of the El Arish border crossing. This is a proud moment for us to welcome visitors across this new border.' Whether he was just being friendly or he wanted a bit more information about me, I don't know, but either way we had a very interesting conversation. He wanted to know all about my plans and told me, 'We are so proud that Egypt has claimed back half of the Sinai Desert.' I left him one of my London postcards.

We four travellers piled into a shared taxi along with three Palestinians. As usual, and as required, there was a period of bargaining, led by the Palestinians, with we backpackers deferring to their expertise. And then we were off into the Sinai. It was a decent tarmac road with sand as far as I could see on either side. Occasionally I saw Bedouins on camels and every so often small groups of simple huts and tent homes. We spoke all the way largely in English. After about three and a half hours we arrived at a spot opposite El Qantara on the Suez Canal, got out of the taxi and waited for the ferry. I sat on the sandy bank and watched a convoy of ships passing slowly down the canal, reminding me that I had been on a ship like these travelling down the Suez four years previously en route to Australia.

The convoy of ships took an hour to pass. It took only a few minutes for the ferry to cross the canal but plenty of time for passengers, cars, lorries, camels, sheep and more to embark and disembark. From there it was another full shared taxi which took a long time to get started, but then we were off to Cairo.

CAIRO

Cairo was vibrant, hot, noisy, congested and enormous. Driving through suburbs was endless and slow but after weeks in the Jordan Valley it was exciting to see so many people, bikes, cars, buses and trucks on the roads and the pavements alive with more people, street food, small fires and shops. Henk and I found a room at the youth hostel on the River Nile in the centre of the city and went to eat in an 'eat all you want' café with huge woks full of different mixes of beans, lentils, rice, grains and vegetables.

The next morning Henk and I went to the Police Headquarters on Tahir Square for the first of many registrations. We then headed off to find the Bazaar but ended up on the edge of the Old City. We sat in a café and looked around. People were really friendly, typically stopping us to say 'Hello', 'Hey Mister', 'From what country?', 'Good morning', and more. We walked around for a while without a map and found another café where we sat outside.

'Welcome to our café,' said a man about my age from the next table. 'My name is Masud and I live here.'

'Thank you. I am Patrick from Britain and this is Henk from the Netherlands,' I replied.

We made our first friend in Cairo. Masud was a student whose parents ran the café. In no time at all we were being introduced to almost everyone in the street. We played Shesh Besh, the backgammon game I'd learned in Jericho, with a retired general called Tawfik. We drank more tea and promised to come back in the evening. We did and had a great night. We sat in the local butcher's shop among all the hanging carcasses of meat and smoked hashish pipes. A few men from the street, including a policeman, came and joined us. It was a very friendly gathering and then we all piled back to the café for tea and Shesh Besh. When we left virtually the whole street said we should come back tomorrow. Of course we did.

The second day in Cairo I went to the British Consulate to request a 'letter of introduction' to the Sudanese Embassy, a vital document. Then off to the café for tea and Shesh Besh, again talking with many of the residents. I had my hair and beard trimmed by Tawfik's barber friend. Henk and I walked a bit around Cairo but came back again to the café.

On the third day I went to the British Consulate to collect my letter of introduction and then to the Sudanese Embassy. I filled in a visa application form.

'May I see your passport?' asked the officer. He examined my main passport which had my Egypt entry stamp. 'Why did you enter Egypt at El Arish?' he demanded. He obviously suspected that I had been in Israel, which would have been the end of my travels south of Egypt. I had to come up with a plausible story on the spot.

'I was on a sailing boat and arrived at El Arish by yacht and walked to the border post.'

He wrote all this down on my application form and then said, 'Come back tomorrow.'

I was calm, but as soon I left the building I started shaking. It was the first time I had lied to an official and was facing a potential end to my journey. I was anxious when I went back to the Sudanese

Embassy the next day. I waited 30 minutes in the queue and when I got to the desk I was presented with my passport with a visa to visit Sudan for one month. I tried hard not to show my relief. My journey would continue.

I met Henk at the hostel and we decided that rather than spend the day at the café today we would wander around old Cairo. It was a really beautiful city, despite its size and chaos. The population of the Greater Cairo metropolitan area was around 7 million in 1980. As of 2024 it is estimated to be over 22 million[4]. Getting around on buses was dangerous. Every bus was packed, with people hanging on to open doors at the back. There was a cacophony of horns. Occasionally we saw traffic cops fighting a losing battle to control the drivers. We walked.

PYRAMIDS

I had been waiting much of my life to visit the Pyramids at Giza. I had saved this day as a treat after the anxiety about my Sudanese visa. We managed to battle our way on to a bus that stopped quite near to the Pyramids. They were magnificent and despite the traders desperate to sell us a camel ride, private tour and souvenirs we managed to walk up to the Great Pyramid, the largest of the three large structures. This was before the days of mass tourism so we were able to join a short queue to climb inside.

The entrance to the passageway was wide but once inside we had to crouch down in a small tunnel, barely wide enough for one person to climb the 130 feet to the main chamber, clambering over or under people returning in the opposite direction. Completing

---

4   ⊘ macrotrends.net/cities/22812/cairo/population

this obstacle course we arrived at a small room with high ceilings. I stood quietly in awe of the experience of being at the heart of this enormous construction as well as thinking about the suffering of the slave labourers who had built it.

Coming out of the dark into the bright sunlight I let my eyes adjust before walking around the Pyramid complex and of course the Great Sphinx of Giza. I'd seen many pictures of this 66-foot-tall limestone statue of a reclining sphinx, a mythical creature with the head of a pharaoh and the body of a lion, but was unprepared for quite how extraordinary it was.

When the sun started to fall, we decided to find something to eat from the small market of tents selling souvenirs and, fortunately, some food. We avoided the many attempts to get us to buy a memento and found a stall selling falafels. Then we sat on a small mound of sand in the desert with a view of the Pyramids and waited for the Son et Lumière show, which we watched for free. The light over the Sphinx was incredible. A day I had waited for since I was a ten-year-old history geek.

After this brilliant day it was back to the mundanity of travelling. I managed to swap my jeans for a pair of light trousers. Those jeans were far too hot for me to wear but probably the most valuable item I owned. Then to the Hilton Hotel to use the toilets and help ourselves to the toilet paper. It was astonishing that the scruffy young man that I was at the time wasn't thrown out. Upon leaving we met an American woman in her 70s who had been at the hotel for the same reason. You could not buy toilet paper in the shops, so it seemed that every traveller went to the Hilton. I dread to think what the hotel budget for toilet paper was. I had yet to manage how to clean up without paper – that would come later.

In the evening Henk and I went back to the café in the square and played Shesh Besh and smoked pipes with some of the older men. Even before we had entered the square they knew we were coming and there were two glasses of *shi*, the local sweet black tea, waiting for us. Our friendly shopkeeper arrived. We explained that we were leaving the next day and I left the café owner and the shopkeeper one of my London postcards each. One was immediately put on the wall above the bar.

OASIS

Henk and I walked to Cairo Railway Station in the morning, arriving in time for the 11:20am train. Then we were ushered into another train. Over the next two hours this train left the station three times only to return each time. Finally, at around 1:30pm, the train left the station. If this had been London the passengers would have been furious but here everyone was happy to be on the train at all. Including the two of us.

The trip was beautiful, passing the Pyramids at Giza and then the Step Pyramid at Saqqara. Alongside the rail track were irrigated fields in the old tradition, little changed since Ancient Egyptian times. Water was raised by oxen-powered wells and hand-turned spiral tubes, which were easily moved to any of the multiple irrigation channels where water was needed. Technology that had endured.

Eventually the train left the valley and passed through empty desert before entering the Faiyum Oasis. We arrived late afternoon and with the help of an elderly man found a hostel to stay in for the minute sum of 40 piastres a night (24 pence in UK currency). We registered with the police and got another stamp in our passports. At this rate I would run out of pages. That evening we ate and sat in cafés playing Shesh Besh. Prices were much cheaper than in Cairo, people were very friendly, and there were few Western travellers.

The next day we took a small local bus. It was a really great way to see the Faiyum Oasis, a basin in the desert to the west of the Nile about 60 miles southwest of Cairo. I enjoyed the beautiful fields, irrigation channels and plenty of tall palm trees of differing varieties. We passed by fields ploughed by oxen and an old brick factory.

Eventually we arrived at the town of Izbat Shakshuk on the shores of the Qarun Lake. There was a lot of flooding on the road but when we arrived it looked really old and peaceful. Except that when we got off the bus we were surrounded by young boys shouting, 'Baksheesh, baksheesh,' meaning 'give us money'. Soon there were maybe 10 of them and some started throwing stones at us. There was a dilemma around giving money to some and not to all. I felt guilty being a Westerner and realised I would have to learn to deal with this feeling. Of course people would assume that we had money and the concept of Westerners with very little money was difficult for people to comprehend.

After giving them a small amount of money we were left alone and walked along the edge of fields of corn and other crops. A farmer gave us a lift on his tractor and then we met three travellers who gave us a lift in their van back to Faiyum. Later that day we all took a local bus to the substantially eroded Pyramid of Amenemhet III. I didn't believe it was a pyramid until we got very close – from afar it looked like a pile of rubble. There are 118 pyramids in Egypt; some are in good condition, while many are piles of stones.

The returning bus stopped in a small village and again we were surrounded by a group of children. No stones were thrown but it was impossible to walk around. A policeman appeared and cleared the children off but then insisted we pay him. I began to realise that I would need to find a way of being helpful rather than just being a tourist with money. It took a while but later in my travels I did find a way. The next day Henk and I took the bus from El Faiyum back to Cairo, driving through desert.

OVERNIGHT TRAIN

The following morning I went to Cairo Station, which was packed with people. I sat waiting for over five hours for the train to appear. Henk had been ill the night before and, uncertain as to whether he could travel, slept in. About an hour before the train arrived, he appeared. When the train arrived it was a fight to get on. People getting off the train had to fight as hard as people getting on, and there were fist fights over seat occupation. To my great surprise I got two seats without being punched and sat down for the 16-hour overnight journey to Luxor. Henk was not feeling good but wanted to get to Luxor, so two fellow passengers helped me heave him up into the luggage rack where he promptly fell asleep.

The train was incredibly crowded and the aisles between seats were filled with people selling food, drinks, fabric and even animals. There was a sense of desperation on the part of the sellers. One man threw blue chewing gum at everyone in the carriage, demanding money from anyone who touched it. He collected most of the gum back from the dirty floor, and I suspected this was thrown again at passengers in the next carriage.

The train journey was long and uncomfortable but never boring. As well as the traders, beggars walked up and down the aisles, pushing their way past passengers as they went. I sat with five other people, eating sugarcane, drinking and talking. Farouk was a police officer travelling back home to Luxor. 'What are you doing travelling in this carriage?' he asked me in English.

'It's all I can afford,' I replied, 'and it's far more interesting.'

He liked that, repeating it in Arabic to the other people sitting nearby who smiled.

After this helpful introduction the journey was great fun. My very basic Arabic was a source of embarrassment to me but no one else seemed to mind. The two men opposite shared their nuts and Coca-Cola, refusing to let me buy anything. The best they let me do was share the small amount of dried fruit and nuts that I brought with me. They argued with each other as to who paid for the next round of food.

The first time the train slowed down to stop at a station, Farouk shouted, 'Lie down!' as everyone in the train ducked down below the open windows above the seats. 'Men selling sugarcane will hurl the thick canes through the windows and come and collect money for this when the train stops at the station. People have been killed in the past by being speared.' And sure enough a few minutes later, what looked like a barrage of canes started flying through these upper windows landing on passengers fortunately not hurting anyone. 'Don't touch them,' shouted Farouk. 'Leave them until the traders come and collect them. If you are holding one when they come you'll have to buy it.'

The train pulled into Luxor station after 16 hours and 400 miles. I was exhausted as I hadn't slept at all. Henk climbed down from the luggage rack having slept the whole way and announced that he felt a bit better. We said goodbye to Farouk and the others after the most fun I'd ever had on a train.

TOMBS

Next morning Henk still had diarrhoea so I got him some bottled water and then set off alone to the Nile, crossing on the locals' ferry, which, amazingly, was free. There was also an elaborate tourist ferry with coaches waiting on the west bank. After I had walked for 30 minutes in 35-degree heat, a man driving a donkey cart stopped and gestured to me to climb in the back. He dropped me at the Colossi of Memnon, two enormous statues of Pharaoh Amenhotep III. I then set off again on foot to the temple of Hatshepsut, which was enormous and built into a cliff. It was breathtaking. Although I had studied the temples and tombs of the Valley of the Kings as a teenage history enthusiast, I had had no idea of their scale.

Coming out of these temples I met Mohammed. He was on his way on foot to the main tombs in the Valley to sell souvenirs. 'Why are you walking? Westerners don't walk here!' he asked me.

'I'm different,' I replied. 'I can't afford the bus and walking is more interesting.'

'Even the Western travellers like you take the bus,' he said. 'Would you like to walk with me?'

Of course I agreed.

'I make a good living selling souvenirs,' Mohammed explained. 'I set my prices by guessing how wealthy each tourist is. I will show you around.'

'I've been looking forward to this day since I was about ten years old,' I told him.

'Then we must make sure that this is a special day,' he replied. And so I found myself with the best tour guide I have ever had. Mohammed took me to each tomb and somehow persuaded the staff to let me in free of charge.

First was the tomb of Ramses IX, which was long and thin with openings along the corridor. The walls were lined with paintings of the king, with symbols describing his life and journey to the afterlife. Then I went to the tomb of Ramses VI, which was similar although longer and the artwork better preserved.

The third tomb was Tutankhamen's. The walls featured simple, colourful paintings around the central sarcophagus, including pictures of the king with various deities, along with the twelve monkeys that are symbolic of the twelve steps to the afterlife.

My next stop was the Tomb of Amenophis. This was deeper than the others and beautifully preserved. The ceiling was blue with yellow stars and the top half of the walls covered with drawings and hieroglyphics in black on a grey background. Nine monkeys featured, with twelve serpents, nine men and twelve gods. There were other drawings of men, boats and various images of burials and religious celebrations. Anubis the Jackal God passed a form of cross to the king, as did other deities. I spent a long time transfixed, imagining the stories that the images depicted. When I emerged, Mohammed asked, 'Why have you been there so long?'

'I've been reading the story of Amenophis in hieroglyphics and pictures,' I replied.

Finally Mohammed took me to the Tomb of Thutmose. The tomb was oval shaped, with yellow walls and black and red line drawings and hieroglyphics. There were many serpents and groups of people – predominantly groups of women but also men, and gods.

As soon as I came out of the last tomb Mohammed appeared again and encouraged me to have a go at trying to get the best price for his souvenirs from the tourists. I wasn't nearly as good at it as him and some of these tourists were insulted and became angry with me. I felt like I had just travelled over thirty centuries in five minutes.

Mohammed was finished working for the day and we walked back towards the ferry together passing a small village where a farmer and his wife and children insisted we come and drink with them. Mohammed translated while they plied me with questions about life in the UK, while the children, chickens and dogs ran around outside their tiny house made largely of reeds. His wife served us a delicious mint tea. I wanted to pay them but Mohammed told me that this would be an insult. Instead I gave them one of my postcards of London which the family gathered around and asked me more questions about. I was glad of my postcard collection. The sun was setting as I gave a postcard to Mohammed and walked back to the ferry.

The next day Henk felt a lot better and we went to the Temple of Karnak. Henk was quite weak and it was over 35 degrees, so it wasn't a long visit. The scale of this temple and the height of the columns were breathtaking. We explored for about an hour and a half, then walked slowly back to our hostel, passing a large funeral procession with nearly one hundred women wailing. We bent our heads in respect as the procession passed and were thanked by two of the men.

LAKE ASWAN

After a third night in Luxor, Henk and I took the train to Aswan, arriving in the late afternoon. The town was clean and modern, with extremely friendly people. We found a hostel to stay in and ate in the 'Palestine Club', which reminded me of the cafés of Jericho. Next morning we went to the Elephantine Island in the middle of the Nile, with its luxury Oberoi hotel built in the 1970s. We took the hotel ferry which was free to guests although I'm not sure how we got away with this. The island accentuated the wealth gap of this part of Egypt. Just next to the opulent hotel was a very poor village. Meanwhile, Aswan seemed to me like a show town. There was a wide road in the centre that came from and led to nowhere. Modern buildings were in abundance with parks and green lawns. It was different to anywhere I'd seen elsewhere in Egypt.

I said goodbye to Henk the next day, handing him letters to post home to my family once he got back to the Netherlands. I felt sad after he left. That evening I went to various cafés, meeting up with backpackers, hoping to find a travelling companion. All were heading back north. I had yet to meet anyone venturing south into Sudan and began to feel anxious as I suspected that travelling would become harder. I had enjoyed the people, the food, the culture and the heritage of Ancient Egypt. Heading south felt like it would be the start of a journey into the unknown – and that felt scary.

With one more day in Aswan, I went to the old town and bought food for the journey, mostly dried fruit, nuts, some flatbread. I had already given up buying drinking water, deciding to trust that my body would adjust to local water. This could have been a mistake but felt like the only realistic option. I had an old army surplus water bottle covered in khaki felt that kept the water cool.

The next morning I took the early train to the Aswan High Dam and the border office. I had to pay for my luggage (virtually none by my travel standards today). I had another discussion about the El Arish stamp in my passport but the officer then waved me through. I hoped that this would no longer be an issue once I had left Egypt. I then joined a huge crowd of passengers attempting to board the third-class section of the ferry.

The ferry was made up of two vessels. The largest, the smart-looking ferry boat, housed the wheelhouse, first-class cabins, dining room and comfortable-looking sunbeds. Its outside decks, covered with awnings, were the domain of Western travellers wearing smart jackets, sun hats and summer dresses. Tied alongside and towering above the ferry boat was a huge barge, which was clearly where everyone else, including me, would travel. This was the third-class (there was no second class) option, with three open-sided decks. Thankfully a roof covered the top, otherwise the strength of the sun would have been unbearable.

I had a fleeting pang of jealousy of those other Western travellers in first class. And then I reminded myself that I wasn't that type of traveller.

I eventually boarded the third-class barge just after 1pm, having stood in the heat of the queue for nearly four hours. There were family groups carrying enormous quantities of luggage and carrier bags, mostly cheaper goods purchased in Egypt to take to Sudan which I was told had few goods in the shops. I helped one family by carrying a couple of bags for them. They expressed surprise that I was carrying so little luggage of my own.

The ferry finally left at around 4pm and began the two-night journey down Lake Nasser, a huge reservoir on the Nile River in Upper Egypt and northern Sudan created by the construction of the Aswan High Dam. The boarding ticket said to arrive at 9am and it had taken all this time to get the hundreds of adults, children, goats, camels, chickens and tons of luggage on to the third-class barge. I settled on the top deck and put my bags down.

'Hello, what is your name?' asked the man next to me. 'I am Faheem and I am going home to Sudan.'

'I'm Patrick from Britain and I'm heading to Swaziland,' I replied.

'That's a long journey,' he said. 'I am studying economics in Egypt.'

'I just finished studying economics,' I said, and suddenly we had plenty in common.

At this point the young man on the other side of me introduced himself with, 'My name is Eshaq and I am going to Sudan for work.'

Once we had started talking I asked, 'Is it safe to leave my possessions here on the deck?'

They both said 'Yes' and Faheem continued, 'Baggage and possessions are safe on the third-class barge the whole journey. Everyone keeps an eye on luggage and if there is any thieving everyone takes care of this.' A fascinating concept that reoccurred throughout my journey.

Faheem and Eshaq took me on a tour of third class. The top deck was largely occupied by solo travellers, the middle deck by families, and the bottom deck was the preserve of camel traders and food stallholders – who cooked on open fires on this largely wooden barge. I was travelling to Sudan on a floating fire hazard. And then there were the toilets. These were pretty grim: basically a hole in the deck that went straight into the lake. By now I was getting used to washing my bottom with water, making sure to only use my left hand, keeping my right hand for eating, as was the etiquette.

Later, after the three of us shared food, Faheem and Eshaq showed me how to climb on to the roof above the top deck. We lay back and looked up at the stars. I couldn't quite believe what I saw.

There were almost more stars than black sky, I had no idea that that many existed. We were crossing the Tropic of Cancer on a moonless night, the stars reflecting on to the still dark waters of the lake. It was an unbelievable sight, not least the almost constant movement of shooting stars, including one that streaked across the sky before breaking up into multiple shards of light. At around 10pm the ferry moored up for the night.

The ferry started again before sunrise. Faheem woke me, suggesting we go back to the roof to watch the light coming up. It was absolutely beautiful. We lay there for a while until the sun started to heat up the roof, and headed to the bottom deck for sweet black coffee. There were camels and their drivers down there, as well as goats and chickens, and the noise and smells were overwhelming.

The views were stunning and in the afternoon I could see the huge statues of the temples at Abu Simbel. Even at a distance they looked impressive. Otherwise it was a lovely slow journey down the lake. I chatted with my companions and other passengers, got up and walked occasionally and slept a bit. Despite the crowding this was a very relaxed way to travel and a gentle transition between Egypt and Sudan.

2

SUDAN

TRAIN ACROSS THE DESERT

The ferry arrived at Wadi Halfa in the north of Sudan mid-morning. There was no sign of a jetty. Small boats sat in the water around the ferry and one of these tied up alongside with some men and equipment. Once they had boarded they started spraying DDT[5] over all the passengers and decks. Everyone wrapped cloth around their faces and mouths, so I quickly grabbed a scarf I'd bought in Cairo and did the same. Today DDT is banned in many countries and there are links to dementia. I'm not sure how effective the scarf was.

After two hours it was announced that they would start to disembark third-class passengers, first class having long since gone. I was one of the first and had to clamber down netting on the side of the third-class barge with my luggage, and jump, or in my case fall, into an unstable dinghy. As I fell the dinghy moved and I ended up half in and half out of the water. Maybe the water washed off the DDT spray, although on the other hand the Nile is renowned for bilharzia, a life-threatening infection caused by a parasitic worm that lives in fresh water in much of Africa[6].

I clambered into the dinghy and grabbed my rucksack as it began to float off. Once on dry land I walked the short distance to the town. Today Wadi Halfa is a small city of over 15,000 people, but then it was a quiet, dusty town with few people around. I sat in

5   epa.gov/ingredients-used-pesticide-products/ddt-brief-history-and-status

6   nhs.uk/conditions/schistosomiasis

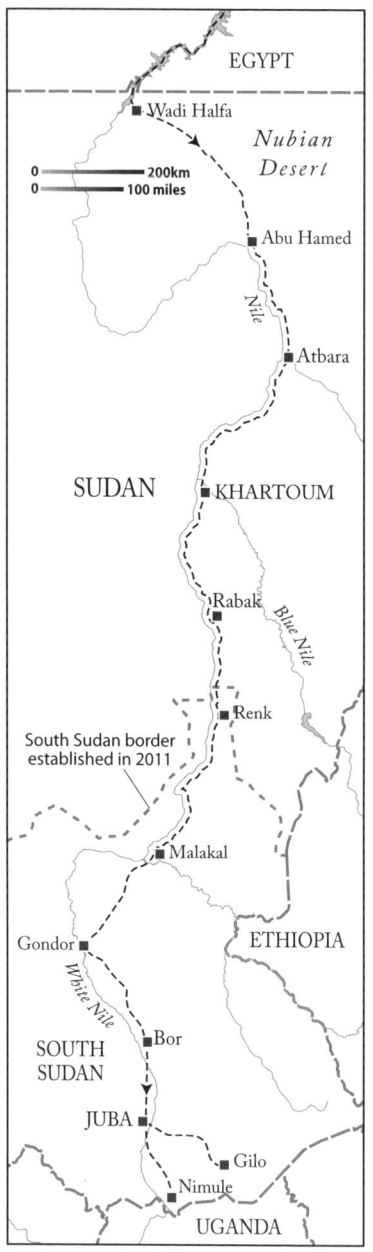

a café drinking coffee and then made my way to the railway station to buy tickets for the train to Khartoum, the only realistic way to travel south.

I had been told I could purchase a student ticket which would give me a discount. And sure enough at the ticket office they confirmed this was the case. Despite the fact that I had already graduated, I still had my student card from Bristol University, which was due to expire at the end of 1980. I bought a third-class ticket and, notwithstanding the large number of passengers (pretty much everyone from the ferry), I managed to find a seat, sitting with five others, including Faheem.

At 6pm the train set off travelling through the Nubian Desert. I must have fallen asleep, as I woke up in the middle of the night. The train had stopped, so I got out at the tiny station and on the platform was immediately served a meal of *ful* and rice washed down with *shi*, the strong and sweet black tea. *Ful* is the most popular dish in Sudan, made from brown beans stewed for hours in a large metal cauldron. The beans are typically partially mashed and served with oil, spices and flatbread called *kisra*. It was the perfect dish for a vegetarian travelling on a tight budget and I would be eating a lot of this.

I fell asleep once I'd got back on the train and woke as the sun rose. We were crossing the Nubian Desert with nothing but sand in every direction and no sign of people or settlements. By mid-morning the train stopped at the station at Abu Hamed where the train tracks rejoined the Nile. There was a small market and I went with some of my travel companions to drink *shi* and buy food for the rest of the journey, mostly fruit and nuts. There were women selling clothes, but I did not buy any.

Later that morning the conductor came along to check the tickets. When he saw mine he asked for my student card and passport. I showed them to him and he started speaking at speed in Arabic. I had some limited understanding of the language at this stage, but he was speaking too fast for me and Faheem translated. The upshot was that the conductor had to keep my passport until we arrived in Khartoum where 'everything would get sorted out'.

I was really anxious about this. The first rule of travelling is never to let anyone take possession of your passport. 'This is not unusual and you should not be concerned,' said Faheem. The truth was that I had no choice but to go along with it. At least I had my second passport, which I had told no one about, hidden – albeit that one had Israeli stamps in it.

After Abu Hamed the train followed the Nile, but unlike in Egypt there was very little fertile land to be seen. There was the occasional village and small town, but the train did not stop for the rest of the day. People outside the train were generally taller than Egyptians, with the women wearing colourful clothing.

KHARTOUM

The train arrived at Khartoum Station at around 3am. The conductor said that he would give my passport to the railway police and I walked with him to their office on the platform. There were police in there but they said that the office would not be open until later when the right officer would arrive. Saying goodbye to Faheem, I slept on the platform outside the office although there was constant activity and sleep was fitful.

Thankfully at 8am I was woken by a police officer with an air of leadership. 'Good morning,' he said. 'We will get your passport back, do not worry.' Fortunately for me, many Sudanese spoke good English.

We walked to the ticket office where we met Karl, a German traveller in the same predicament. The upshot was that the ticket office did not recognise the validity of my student card and I had to pay extra for the ticket from Wadi Halfa. Although this blew my budget for the week, I got my passport back. I made a mental note to never let it out of my sight again. The police officer was really kind and stayed to negotiate all this with the ticket office manager.

'Come with me for *shi*,' said the officer. We sat in his office and he explained some of the complexities of travelling in Sudan. 'Although you have a visa, you must always visit the police station in every town you spend the night for them to stamp your passport.' 'Where do you intend to travel to after Khartoum?' he then asked.

'Juba,' I replied.

He took a sharp intake of breath. 'It's a dangerous place,' he said. 'Why do you want to go there?'

I explained about my overland journey to Swaziland.

'There is fighting in Juba and there is cholera,' he replied. 'You will need to go to the central police station and get permission to travel to Juba. They may not give this to you. Are you sure you want to go there?'

He was so helpful and friendly and, despite my heart sinking, I appreciated him being so straightforward with me. He was thrilled when I gave him one of my London postcards. He brought out a small business card in Arabic and English and explained that this had his name and contact details. He insisted that I showed this to any police officer I saw along my travels. A very kind gesture.

Karl and I went into Khartoum and found accommodation at a small hostel. The beds were outside on a patio with shading, very necessary in 40-degree heat. It was easy to hitchhike around the city so we got a lift to a small café and enjoyed sandwiches and juices. By late morning it was so incredibly hot, and someone suggested going to the United States Cultural Centre which had air conditioning. That was a massive relief although I realised that I would need to get used to the heat.

That night I had my first dysentery of the journey. It wasn't too uncomfortable but I didn't eat any food the next day and by the middle of the afternoon was feeling better. I found the Central Post Office, which was nearby, and collected four letters from Poste Restante: two from my dad, one from my mum and one from my friend James. This was a treat and while I was still at the post office I wrote each of them a letter on the old blue aerogrammes.

Poste Restante was a service for travellers who didn't have a permanent address but still wished to receive mail. On my journey it was generally only provided by the main capital city post offices, which were few and far between. It appears to be still available today despite the fact that most travellers can now stay in touch with home via smartphones or email. It was important for me and I read the letters I'd received a few times each.

Later I went to the Central Police Station to register and to fill in a form to apply to travel to Juba. Given the amount of bureaucracy involved in being a backpacker in Sudan, this was surprisingly straightforward but I had to come back the next day to collect the permit.

Karl discovered that the university had a swimming pool. My UK student card gave me access, which was really brilliant, so finally I had some use for it. We spent the afternoon by the pool, swimming and lounging. I needed to relax, partly because of my very mild dysentery, but as I lay on a sunbed by the pool I made a mental note to do this as often as I could. Travelling was not relaxing – although in the end the previous four weeks would prove to have been some of the easiest of the whole journey.

I had a great night's sleep, despite the humidity. My stomach had returned to normal and the next morning I went to get some *ful* and flatbread which I ate gently and slowly. At the Central Police Station my permit for travel to Juba was ready. I had heard stories from other travellers, ranging from days of waiting to receiving an outright refusal, so it was a real surprise to get mine so easily. I went to seek out the Ugandan Embassy, as I would need a visa to cross the border in the south. To my surprise they were closed on a Sunday. I had adjusted to the Muslim Friday/Saturday weekend in Egypt and Sudan and hadn't remembered that, as a largely Christian country, Uganda would take Sunday off.

I walked around this hot and dusty city, coming to the point where the River Nile is joined by its two major tributaries, the White Nile that flows from Lake Victoria and Blue Nile that flows from the Ethiopian mountains. The White Nile is rich in light grey sediments while the Blue Nile has its darker colour due to the heavy silt it carries.

The next day I heard again that there was a cholera epidemic in Juba. I had planned to travel as far as I could down the White Nile, but that wasn't going to happen as the boats had been stopped. The alternative would be to go overland, travelling on a goods vehicle. I had no idea whether this was possible and as always there were different stories told by different travellers and officials. I went to the University Club and discussed this with a group of travellers there. There was some talk of travelling together to Port Sudan and getting a boat to Mombasa on the Kenyan coast, which was viable as this was long before the days of pirate activity off the coast of Somalia.

An alternative was to travel overland through Ethiopia, but this was dangerous. Ethiopia had seen conflict for a long time and there were some Ethiopian refugees in the hostel who told some pretty terrible tales. I would have loved to travel through Ethiopia. It sounded like a beautiful country with wonderful people and a rich culture, but I didn't think I was prepared to take the risk.

By the end of the discussion, two of the group had decided to travel overland to Port Sudan and try and get a boat, and the third was undecided. I went back to the hotel and for once in my life decided to sleep on it. I'm generally a quick decision-maker, but this was too important to rush.

Travelling by sea to Kenya was appealing but would almost certainly cost quite a bit and seriously eat into my meagre budget. Also, I had set myself the target of travelling overland to Swaziland and this would be a significant change. But travelling through Ethiopia was just too dangerous. I accepted that there would be a level of danger in my journey south but heading knowingly into what sounded like a civil war was a step too far.

That left me one option, which was to see if I could hitch a lift on a goods lorry to Juba, or at least part of the way. By the end of the evening I decided that I would head for the lorry park in the morning and try to find a lorry driver prepared to take me south.

I got up early and went to the lorry park at Souk Shabi in Omdurman, the city across the Nile from Khartoum. It was a huge, dusty area with about a hundred lorries surrounded by market stalls selling food and drink, clothing, spare engine parts for lorries, tyres, oil and diesel and much more. I spent two hours walking from lorry to lorry asking drivers where they were travelling to and, if heading south, whether they would be prepared to give me a lift. Not many were heading south. They had all heard about the cholera and there was clearly a lot of debate among drivers as to how safe heading south would be.

By mid-morning I wasn't feeling confident that I could get a ride. The lorry park was starting to clear, with drivers heading off, either on a new job or home for the day. I was just about to leave when I spotted a lorry with '*Sudan Council of Churches, Relief*

Programme Gift from CWS' written on the side[7]. I walked over and started talking to the two drivers.

'Where are you heading to?' I asked.

'We are hoping to go as far as Renk,' one of the men replied. 'Are you wanting to travel there too?'

'I am hoping to get to Juba,' I replied. 'Would you be able to take me to Renk with you?'

Today Renk is the border town where you cross from Sudan to the new nation of South Sudan (created in 2011). Although it is only about 450 miles from Omdurman, it was a dusty and often rutted track for most of the way. It would be a day and a half's drive to get there.

'We are leaving tomorrow morning,' said one of the men, whose name was Aziz. 'Come and meet us here at five o'clock in the morning. Bring some food and water. And make sure that you bring a headscarf as it will be dusty.'

I thanked them, bought some dried fruit, nuts and flatbread from the stalls, and headed back to Khartoum.

Back in the city I went again to the University Club. I sat down with Irshad, a politics student who was very keen to educate me about the recent political history of Sudan. 'In 1969, a military coup put President Nimeiry in power, but despite his leadership there is constant conflict between the military and civil elites and there is the threat of another coup. Have you ever had a military coup in your country?'

---

7   CWS is the Church World Service. As a severe famine swept through Ethiopia and
     the rest of the Horn of Africa in the 1980s, the CWS mobilised a relief effort of over
     US$17 million.

Irshad continued to give me his assessment of the challenges facing Sudan. I largely listened and was a little wary of sharing any opinions. He covered a lot of ground. Relations between the north and south of the country were improving but the south was virtually a different country. There was a lot of dissatisfaction with the government as the only option on election ballots was the Sudanese Socialist Union, the governing party. The bureaucracy was led by the military and was complex and time-consuming for the majority of citizens.

ROUGH TRAVELLING

At 5am the next morning I was at the lorry park at Souk Shabi where I found Aziz and Kazim, his co-driver. The lorry was a flatbed with sacks of food aid packed to the top of the high sides, about 10 feet above the ground. The sacks were tied tightly with ropes and about 15 people were already sitting on top. Two of them helped me climb up.

The sun had only been up for an hour and by the time we set off it was already very hot. I wore a scarf on my head covering most of my face, as did everyone else. One of the men showed me how to tie my small rucksack on to the ropes on the top of the sacks and how to get comfortable sitting on a sack with my legs over the side of the lorry. I held on to the ropes with both hands and it was surprisingly comfortable. Once we started moving it was cooler.

About an hour into the journey we were driving through desert when the lorry ground to a halt. The fan buckled and split the radiator. Aziz and Kazim, who were clearly excellent mechanics, removed the radiator. There were a number of lorries driving in both directions so they waved one down and Kazim hitched a ride carrying the broken radiator. Aziz waited with us passengers.

This would clearly take some time so everyone climbed down from the top of the lorry and walked around a bit. About 30 minutes later there was a commotion and everyone slid underneath the lorry. I quickly followed, wrapping my scarf around the whole of my head and face, copying what the others were doing. That was just in time as within minutes a cloud of sand encircled the lorry and swept through the underside where we were all gathered. I lay on the ground taking short breaths, trying not to inhale the sand as it swirled around. It was a sandstorm and all I could see through the gauze of my scarf were bodies covered in sand.

It felt like a long time but after an hour the storm passed. Everyone emerged from underneath and we moved away from each other and shook ourselves and our clothes until most of the sand had fallen away. After three hours Kazim returned with a replacement radiator and he and Aziz took another hour to put it back. By now it was late morning and approaching the heat of the day, but despite this they were very efficient and appeared to enjoy their work. They kept asking me and other passengers to come and observe their impressive mechanical skills.

Once the job was completed everyone climbed back on to the top of the lorry and we set off through the sandy desert punctuated by only the occasional withered shrub. Every so often there was a shout from one of the drivers and the lorry stopped. We climbed down from the top of the lorry and dug the wheels out of the sand. There was no road as such, just a track in the sand that other lorries had used, but there were areas of soft sand slowing the journey. No one seemed at all concerned about this and I found myself questioning why I was always in a hurry back home. Each time we stopped Kazim got down one of the jerrycans of water and topped up the radiator, taking no chances.

After some hours we rejoined the bank of the river and passed through green scrubland and many small villages. Then we were back in the desert, although this time there was some vegetation. It reminded me of parts of the Australian outback, where I'd travelled four years previously. I saw beautiful geese, quail and some very large birds whose name I did not know.

There were stops on the way with small cafés and places to sit in the shade. I was eating *ful* pretty much every meal. Occasionally the cafés would serve meat, which was very popular with the drivers and the majority of the passengers, but *ful* was what I liked. There would be many times over the rest of the journey when I would dream of a plate of it.

We carried on driving after sunset and finally arrived at Rabak at around 9pm. Rabak is a town on the banks of the White Nile which at the time had a population of around 25,000. It is now a small city of over 150,000 and an industrial centre. After a long day mostly driving through desert and the occasional village, it felt quite different to stop in a town this large. I was tired and settled down to sleep under the lorry.

I loved travelling through Egypt and the north of Sudan, but this was the first day I felt like my overland travels had truly begun. I had spent the day with a group of Sudanese travelling the only way that was available to them. It was hot, bumpy, often uncomfortable and slow. I was the only Western traveller on the lorry and saw no others. I spoke rudimentary Arabic and some of my fellow passengers spoke some English. They had told me about the people in the villages we had passed through, how they made their living and more. I was perceived as unusual as a Westerner travelling in the same way as local people travelled. As a white man from a wealthy country I was – and am – privileged compared to everyone I met on my journey. What I found was the more I travelled, ate and slept with the people I met, the less of a barrier there was that this privilege often creates.

I woke up early after a good sleep underneath the parked lorry, wedged in between fellow passengers. The next day I enjoyed even more. The view from the top of the lorry was spectacular, passing through many small villages with round homes made of straw and mud and sometimes the smoke from a fire. Most of the people I saw farmed cotton and reared cattle, goats, water buffalo and sheep.

Despite the intense heat, travelling on the top of the lorry was cooler and I learned to sit comfortably on sacks for hours at a time. The minute the lorry stopped I'd immediately feel the 40-degree heat. I needed my headscarf, making a mental note to buy a second one as backup. I wore a thin long-sleeved shirt and trousers. My co-passengers wore light cotton *djellabas*, the long, loose-fitting unisex outer robe or dress with full sleeves worn across much of North Africa. It's extremely practical in the heat and I needed to get one of these as soon as possible.

In mid-morning I saw the first of many refugee camps. It was small and although we did not stop there, I was told that the people were mostly Ethiopians who had fled the seemingly endless wars in their country. The Ethiopian Civil War was fought between the Ethiopian military junta and Ethiopian-Eritrean anti-government rebels from 1974 to 1991 with the result that huge numbers of people fled to neighbouring countries and eventually across much of the Western world. At the time I was in Sudan the country's refugee population was officially estimated at 460,000.

After midday we arrived at Renk. We parked up in the lorry park where Aziz and Kazim would unload the food aid before returning to Khartoum. Aziz had a few conversations with other drivers and then came to me saying, 'I have arranged a ride for you to Juba with another lorry.'

I said goodbye to Aziz and Kazim and the passengers. There was much wishing me good luck for my journey from all of them and as much appreciation from me as I could muster in my limited Arabic.

I was beginning to understand that people wanted to help me on my journey and the more I talked about it the more people were interested. I had become another traveller on the top of a lorry, sharing food and water, hiding from sandstorms and hanging on to stop falling. And I had been told a few times that it was good that I didn't have a camera, that this was respectful.

SURVIVAL

I met the new driver, Mohmadi, whose English was good. I sat with him and some of his passengers at a *shi* stall inside a smoky bamboo hut with two women serving from a large pot sitting on a charcoal stove.

'Do you know where Idi Amin is?' asked Mohmadi.

'I have no idea,' I replied.

'I'm sure that the British Government knows where he is,' he responded.

'If they do, they haven't told me yet.'

He laughed and we carried on talking about Uganda. When I told him I planned to go there he was horrified. 'Uganda is very dangerous – you must be careful.' Mohmadi then changed the subject, telling me that it would be a three-day journey to Juba. We set off later that afternoon.

This lorry ride was different from the last one. The baggage was piled very high, well above the top of the driver's cabin. I perched on the edge of two sacks and most of that afternoon and evening was terrified that I would fall off. Survival took up all of my mental energy. Due to the height I felt the bumps in the track a lot more; it was a mostly rutted track so the lorry shook much of the time. I gripped the ropes very tightly and got blisters on my hands. My body was numb, which was perhaps a good thing as I felt less.

At around midnight the lorry stopped at a town called Paloich in a tiny lorry park. I was really relieved as the last few hours had been an ordeal. Given the shifting around of my fellow passengers I wasn't the only person struggling to find some form of comfort on this journey. Over time I began to get better at sitting on a bumpy lorry for hours on end. But most of all I felt that I was finally sharing the experience of Sudanese travellers. It was an exhausting, exhilarating and humbling feeling.

At sunrise we set off again, with a short stop at a tiny village for *shi*, essential for everyone on the lorry, especially Mohmadi and his co-driver and mechanic Ahmed. The lorry was incredibly tough, which it had to be due to the rough and mostly rutted road. Steel formed the suspension with solid blocks of timber on top. Resting on the timber there was a metal casing and frame which rose about 15 feet above the timber and all the sacks of grain packed tightly inside this with ropes over the top to hold them in. And us passengers sitting on top hanging on for dear life. The engine was large and built to last. Mohmadi and Ahmed told me that they drove down to Juba one week and back to Khartoum the next, doing this pretty much all year, even during Ramadan. That's 1,144 miles each way, so about 60,000 miles a year. That might not sound much by UK standards, but on dusty, rutted tracks it was an incredible feat for that lorry and those two amazing drivers.

Little did I then know that within a year I would be driving a lorry and doing about the same mileage per year, albeit on motorways and tarmac roads. Whenever I complained about traffic and other hold-ups I would remind myself of Mohmadi and Ahmed.

This was another tough day of travelling. I kept having to shift my body on top of the sacks just to stay comfortable. Sometimes I had cramp but obviously couldn't walk around, which would be the usual remedy. I had to find a way of staying in the same position. This was a largely mental exercise that some years later I would have called meditation, but at this point it was a form of survival. Maybe this is why I have always struggled with meditation.

The drive from Paloich to the Malakal ferry took about six hours. It was incredibly bumpy. But it was also incredibly beautiful. I'd left North Africa and entered the centre of the continent. There were more villages and I saw, and sometimes met, mostly very tall male hunters carrying spears and shields and tall women typically carrying loads of firewood or water for long distances. These were Dinka people, an ethnic group native to South Sudan and making up 40% of the population. Most of the men and women had closely cropped black hair, sometimes with scars on the head, and wore clothing from the waist downwards, usually a piece of fabric. Men's average height was six foot four inches, women's six foot. My fellow passengers on the top of the bumpy lorry included an old man with white hair and a blind woman. There was a pride about these people that I had not experienced before. Meeting them was humbling and I realised that I needed to stop feeling so self-absorbed. I had an easy and privileged life and made the choice to travel as I did.

As we approached Malakal it became clear that there was an election, with posters up in all the villages as we got closer to the town. These were typically stuck on to almost every tree, particularly the 'village tree' that sat in the middle of each of the tiny villages we passed through. We arrived at the Malakal ferry in the mid-afternoon and crossed the river. Surprisingly there was hardly any wait for the ferry to arrive for the short, slow crossing. Mohmadi drove on to a small flatbed barge that took two lorries at a time with a tug tied alongside that powered the barge across the river.

Malakal was the site of a tragic ferry disaster in 2014. Two hundred women and children drowned when their overloaded boat capsized on the Nile as they scrambled to escape fighting in the town. With hindsight, I realised that I had been travelling in a time of relative peace, although there was obvious tension between the northern and southern parts of Sudan, which I picked up in snippets of conversations.

The next morning was the fourth day of the journey from Khartoum to Juba. A lot had changed for me in these four days. I was travelling with Sudanese people, eating with them, sharing discomfort and learning about their country and lives. I looked at my map that morning and worked out that I had travelled about 2,200 miles since I'd left the Jordan Valley. I sat on the top of the lorry feeling more comfortable as my body adjusted to the shapes of the sacks and the bumpiness of the road. I had a great view of the country we were travelling through but at the same time had to watch out for overhanging trees when all passengers would duck down and lie very close to one another until we had passed them. A branch could knock one or more of us off the lorry – or worse.

A GREAT HONOUR

Around midday we stopped in a small Dinka village comprising three huts, about 20 people and millions of flies. Trying to stop the flies landing on me was impossible. The men and women each wore a single piece of cloth tied over one shoulder and hanging right down almost to the ground. Most of the small boys running around wore no clothes at all, with their bodies streaked with dust. They seemed impervious to the flies. Mohmadi announced that we would stop here for a couple of hours and despite my instant panic at the thought of two hours sitting in a cloud of flies, I found that after a while I noticed them less and allowed them to sit on me and get tangled up in my hair.

There was some food being cooked for us, which enabled the villagers to earn some money. The smoke of the fire helped keep the flies away and I moved closer to it. Mohmadi was speaking to a small group of men from the village and came over to me.

'The village has never had a Westerner stop here on a lorry,' he said. 'They would like to speak with you.' Of course I said yes. Mohmadi told me he would do his best to translate, which he did. The village elders wanted to know all about where and why I was travelling. I told them I was heading to Swaziland to visit a friend. They did not know where that was so I got a stick and drew a map of the African continent in the dust and showed them the route of my journey.

There was much talking among the elders and by now others had arrived, including some of the women and children. Eventually the elders spoke with Mohmadi again and he told me, 'They are keen to offer you a special delicacy with dinner. This is a great honour and you must accept this.'

I was instantly anxious. I have had a lifelong hatred of eating meat and although I had eaten some from time to time, I always felt ill afterwards. But there was nothing to be done. I asked Mohmadi if he knew what this delicacy would be and he replied that he did not.

Dinner arrived, which was goat meat and beans in a stew. I could manage beans and so far on the trip no one had been offended by my eating just the beans from a stew. However, before the main meal could be eaten, the elder came up to me and presented me with a very small, steaming item. It was a sheep's eye. I have rarely been so horrified in my life and hoped that it wouldn't show. I had to smile, say 'Thank you' and somehow eat the eye, with the whole village looking on. It was slimy, fortunately very small, and I shut my eyes as I placed it in my mouth.

To this day I don't know how I managed to do this without throwing up, but somehow I did. I feel sick just thinking about it more than 40 years later. I washed the eye down quickly, drinking the entire contents of my water bottle. There were a few moments where I struggled to avoid vomiting and retain my composure and then I bowed to the elders. They smiled and there was again much talking. I felt like this was some rite of passage but clearly it was a great honour. No one laughed; it was all very serious. I felt a certain respect from my co-passengers. Mohmadi was clearly pleased. I reached into my bag and solemnly handed a postcard of Tower Bridge to the Dinka elders, the only item of any value that I had to offer.

WATER AND FAMINE

After the honour of the sheep's eye, we drove off again, passing through dusty land with more trees as we went further south. Many of the trees looked red due to the bark peeling off in the heat. The palette was a mixture of green, brown and red.

As darkness fell there was a bit of a fight on the top of the lorry. I tried to stay out of it but that was difficult. The long journey and the general discomfort were getting to everyone. But mostly the lack of sleep. Everyone, including me, was finding it impossible to sleep at night because it was too dangerous to let go of the ropes. And we had not been able to top up with water anywhere since lunchtime and were all dehydrated. Tempers were fraught but survival vital on a moving, bumpy lorry so after a few minutes everyone calmed down.

At around two in the morning the lorry drew up at a waterhole, which was surrounded by a crowd of maybe 100 people. I started to climb down and tripped on a side rope and fell. It wasn't a huge fall but enough to wind me and give me a few bruises. I was so tired and desperate for water, but so was everyone around the waterhole. 'With this many local people trying to get water from the well, we don't stand a chance,' said Mohmadi. 'We will stop for the rest of the night and see how things are in the morning.' So although we could not get water, we could get some sleep, and I joined the rest of the passengers as we lay on the ground underneath the lorry.

The next morning I woke with the sun and went to the waterhole with my empty water bottle. There was still a large crowd of people gathered around it and as far as I could see there were people walking here from all directions. It was clearly the only functioning waterhole for miles around. I was standing just outside the crowd, looking forlorn. I was about to turn away when a small boy came up to me and gestured for me to give him my water bottle. I decided to trust him and handed it over. He disappeared into the crowd and was back about 10 minutes later, handing me my bottle full of water. I was speechless but thanked him as best I could, reaching into my backpack and offering him the remains of the large bag of peanuts I'd bought in Khartoum. It was all the food I had but I reckoned that it was a fair exchange. He was thrilled and with a smile dashed off with the nuts. I shared my water with everyone on the lorry, each of us having a small sip. It was just enough.

The lorry set off and we soon arrived in Gondor. I was the most tired I'd ever felt, so it was a minor miracle when we stopped at a *shi* stall. I drank six small cups in quick succession. That felt better. Gondor was a relatively large village and had a policeman who escorted Mohmadi and all us passengers to the well to fill up our bottles with water. The lorry park was busy and I met a trader from the north who offered me breakfast, but Mohmadi was about to leave.

We carried on south towards Juba. There were many villages full of hordes of naked children running alongside the lorry. Often they seemed scared of the white man and ran off. Other times they would laugh at me while I communicated by pulling funny faces. But it was very obvious that these children were hungry. Even the young ones were hunting and if they saw a discarded can they would lick out the remaining contents. Even empty cigarette packets were licked out. There was famine here; what I didn't know then was that this was the beginning of the Ethiopian famine, a humanitarian disaster in which one million people died, and which led to the displacement of millions who ended up as refugees. I did not know the scale of this at the time but understood better when

BBC reporter Michael Buerk brought stories and images from a feeding site to UK television sets in October 1984. But even when I was in Sudan I realised that this was a serious situation and felt helpless. I sometimes wondered if it was a mistake, my travelling here. I was one more mouth.

We carried on and after the small town of Bor the road improved considerably and more patches of water began to appear. The trees and shrubs were greener and larger. There were lots of gazelle and water buffalo close to the road and occasional rainfall for a few minutes. The first in a long time. We eventually stopped in the town of Mongalla for the night. Because of the requirement to register at the police station, I got to meet a lot of police officers who were mostly helpful and friendly towards me. At that time, a Western traveller on the lorries was pretty rare, so a registration was an event and involved multiple cups of *shi* and sometimes food and conversations. There was a less positive side to the police presence, however, which was significant. Most of the officers were from the north of Sudan and were there to stop uprisings from the people of the south. As we got nearer to Juba there were many more police everywhere, most of whom carried guns.

I learned that when Britain was the colonial power it prioritised the development of the Arabic north over the Black African south. This imbalance continued after Sudan gained independence in 1956, leading to a lengthy civil war that was only resolved with autonomy for the south in 2005 and independence in 2011. Sadly this did not end conflict in the new Republic of South Sudan, which, as of 2024, is the poorest country in the world [8].

---

8   *⌀* gfmag.com/data/economic-data/poorest-country-in-the-world

Fighting reignited in Khartoum in 2023, primarily between the army chief, who is head of state, and the paramilitary Rapid Support Forces. As I write, this has now spread across much of the country. Both countries' populations have suffered over many years while these conflicts get very little attention from the rest of the world. I find this shocking.

JUBA

The next morning we drove the last 50 miles into Juba. On the way I saw beautiful spiky-leaved trees with huge fruits on them. I'd never seen or eaten a papaya before. They were everywhere.

The lorry journey had been incredible but very challenging. I was exhausted but at the same time exhilarated. I had never done a journey like this before. It was hard and physically taxing. I had met extraordinary people and been welcomed and supported by them. I had seen famine and experienced lack of water, albeit for only a day. I had received a great honour from a Dinka community and managed not to embarrass myself or them.

We arrived in the lorry park mid-morning and it was time to say goodbye to my fellow passengers. The lorry park was huge, with maybe 40 lorries and the crews sitting around cooking or sleeping. Almost every vehicle was being repaired, with the drivers and mechanics typically fixing the suspensions which took a hammering over the bumpy and rutted road from Khartoum.

At one end of the lorry park was the *souk* (market). There were small *shi* and food stalls. South Sudanese cuisine is based on grains (maize and sorghum), and it uses yams, potatoes, vegetables, beans, lentils, peanuts, meat (goat, mutton, chicken), okra and fruit as well. I was delighted to find *ful* here and it was the nicest I had eaten yet, made with fava beans, ground cumin, fresh herbs and a zippy lemon garlic sauce.

Alongside was the fruit market where I ate the first mango of my life. Never having seen a mango in 1970s Britain, I ate the whole thing in one go, which was a taste explosion. There were also papaya, bananas, cucumbers and some other fruit and vegetables, although for a town the size of Juba, there was not a huge amount of food for sale.

Next to the market was the police complex. This comprised offices, the jail, customs and a variety of buildings. A wall surrounded the complex, with large, guarded gates and barbed wire on the top. It reminded me of Northern Ireland, where my family spent most summer holidays visiting relatives. I had to go inside to get my passport stamped, which although relatively simple was a chilling experience. I had to walk past the jail and could see emaciated men jammed in cells with many pushed against the windows which consisted of bars across a hole in the wall. I guessed this was deliberately set up as a reminder that the police were all-powerful in this part of the country. It served its purpose for me and I assume others who entered the compound.

I walked back to the lorry park to say a final goodbye to Mohmadi and Ahmed. They were having a day off driving before loading up that evening for the journey back to Khartoum. They insisted that they show me where I should stay while in Juba: the Africa Hotel. This sounded like an establishment that would be priced beyond my budget but Ahmed insisted it would be fine and that young Western travellers like me stayed there. He was right; there was a long corridor at the back of the hotel lined with beds. It was a dormitory-style hostel – just a bed, mosquito net and a locker for luggage. A large poster announced the rules of the hotel. No alcohol, no drugs, no gambling and more. I paid for a bed for three nights and sadly said goodbye to Mohmadi and Ahmed, thanking them for taking such good care of me and giving them each a London postcard.

I lay down on my bed and fell asleep immediately. I must have been asleep all afternoon when I woke up to someone gently shaking me.

'Wake up! Let's go and find something to eat,' said a British voice.

'Who are you?' I asked in a dreamy manner.

'I'm Rob. I've just arrived by lorry from Khartoum.'

'Me too,' I said. 'I've barely slept for five days. I'm Patrick.'

I dragged myself up from my bed and Rob and I walked to the *souk* to get some food. As we walked rain started to pour down. We ran into a small stall with lots of other people and ate there. The stallholders could not believe their luck with so many customers arriving at once. It was good to see rain again.

That night I had my first proper sleep in a week. The next day Rob and I spent the afternoon together. We took a ride across the river in a dugout canoe made of a tree trunk and on the other side walked around the small villages. Many people were interested in us and we spoke with them. It was mostly women doing the work, picking mangoes and papayas, distilling spirit from fruit and cleaning. The villages and huts were immaculately tidy. Children appeared less frightened than those I had encountered on the journey here and better fed too. Some of the villages had small schools.

Most of the beds in the hotel dormitory were occupied by refugees from Ethiopia. That evening we cooked a meal of beans and vegetables on Rob's small pot, which we shared with Kebede, Kofi and Neberu, three Ethiopian students who had fled oppression there. 'Soldiers came to our university and said that we had to leave,' said Kebede. 'We were fearful for our lives and came here.'

'We crossed the border and expected to get papers from the United Nations,' said Neberu. 'But we can't get these and now the police here are harassing us.'

'What do you plan to do?' I asked.

'We have been told by the United Nations office that we can enter Kenya and so we plan to travel overland there,' said Kofi.

The conversation carried on late into the evening. They told us a lot about how difficult it had been for them. I had thought my travelling here was challenging but it was nothing compared to what these men, about my age, had endured. Despite this they remained positive and were determined to find somewhere to complete their studies.

I felt – and hope I adequately communicated – such great respect for the students' attempts to find somewhere safe where they could live, study and work. Interestingly I found that respect reciprocated. Towards the end of the evening I asked, 'What do you think about Westerners like us travelling here?'

The three of them started laughing. 'Of course we are happy to see you here, you take an interest in us and hopefully you will tell people our story.'

Many years later in London I was approached to employ an Ethiopian trade union leader who had escaped likely imprisonment or death. I gave him a job which allowed him and his family to settle in the UK.

Rob left the next morning, heading overland to Kenya. We'd had some great chats including about his time working at Suma, a workers' co-operative selling wholefoods. Little did I then know how significant this conversation would turn out to be. We agreed to meet up in Lamu on the Kenyan coast, but I knew that these agreements to meet up rarely happened on journeys like ours.

I had heard about the Imatong Mountains to the east of Juba and particularly a place called Gilo that sounded beautiful. I had done a lot of travelling and wanted to go somewhere to relax, surrounded by nature. But before I could do this, I had to get permission, which meant another trip to the police. Explaining why I wanted to travel to Gilo wasn't easy. I spoke with the 'Captain' twice that morning and my passport visited him three times. I worked out how the system worked – all applications for travel were put on a pile on the Captain's desk and when he left the room, which he did frequently, the trick was to put mine on the top of the pile. And keep smiling and laughing. Eventually I got my stamp.

MOUNTAIN RETREAT

In the morning I went to the bus stop in Juba. I needed to travel to Torit, a town 85 miles away by road. By the time I got there I had missed the bus, but almost immediately was offered a lift by Garang who was really delightful. He took me to visit his father-in-law in his village where I was offered a spirit called *warega* to drink. It was vile but by now I'd learned that it was important to accept any gift graciously, smiling and working hard not to show my disgust. It was better than the sheep's eye.

Garang kindly dropped me at the local police station where I waited three hours for a bus that never came. As ever, the police were friendly and offered me *shi*, which in the heat was really welcome. Hot drinks were the best option in this climate; they lead the body to sweat faster, getting rid of excess heat far more efficiently than a cold drink.

Eventually a car stopped and Godwin offered me a lift. 'I would like to introduce you to my family,' he said.

'Thank you, I would be honoured,' I replied, and that's what we did.

When we arrived in Torit we went to his family home where they offered me a drink called *diuc*, a type of beer made of honey, and *pivinda*, a dip made of peanuts. To my relief, both were delicious. We then walked around the village as Godwin introduced me to his friends and tasted a different homemade drink at each of their homes. Fortunately they were small drinks, as I was not used to alcohol any more. My favourite was *conimro*, made of sesame. That night I slept at Godwin's family compound, among the huts, falling asleep looking up at the stars.

Godwin was funny and highly perceptive, spotting the slightest uneasiness in anyone. He spoke a lot about the recent civil war between North and South Sudan in which his father and brother were both killed. 'I fear that there is another war coming,' he said, and talked about secret arms and drug deals supplying and funding the various militia as well as the police and army.

The next morning Godwin drove me to the town of Katire, where I bought food in the market: beans, nuts, dried fruit, vegetables and some herbs. I said goodbye to him there and managed to hitch a lift up to Gilo in a company Land Rover. Just as well, as it was a very steep climb up to the Imatong Mountains on a tiny track of a road. As we climbed it became noticeably cooler, which felt good.

Gilo was a former colonial hill station, where British colonial officials and their families used to stay to escape the heat. I stayed at the Government Rest House, which was old and musty. After travelling through Egypt and Sudan, this was the perfect place to relax. There was a kitchen where I could cook and a beautiful lounge with a log fire that the aged caretaker lit every night. I slept in a bed with sheets for the first time in a long while and there was a bath with hot water. I soaked in this for an hour when I arrived, washing off the sand and dirt of weeks of travel. Luxury for less than a dollar a day.

This was another world after weeks of heat, dust and flies. All around were forests and hills with beautiful walks and mountain streams that I was told were safe for swimming. I spent the next day walking through thick forest, tall trees and dense green undergrowth. After a couple of hours, I stopped by a small stream and sat in the cool water before arriving in an open, grassy and rocky clearing. From here a valley descended and beyond were hills covered in trees. All I could hear were the sounds of insects, birds and running water, with no visible signs of human life. I sat for a while drinking in the beauty of it all, then climbing higher to see an incredible view down the valley below. To the south I could see Uganda. Everywhere around were mountains, trees and huge rocky outcrops. Immediately below was a tiny village of huts on a small hill in a clearing. I walked down and said hello to some of the villagers who offered me water. After spending a little time sitting with them, I headed back into the forest in the direction of the guest house, using a compass and a map I'd borrowed. The forest became quite thick and at some points the bushes closed in on the path and towered above me. Many of the trees were bent into contorted shapes with huge forms growing from their branches. At another stop I tried to light a cigarette but the match burned out before there was a flame – the air was thinner than I realised. I got back to the guest house late afternoon. I had walked almost all day and was tired and hungry, realising how unfit and weak I was.

I woke up the next morning out of food and set off walking down the road to the town. About halfway down the hill I met the caretaker. I joined him and together we bounded down the steep road at speed. In the town I bought plenty of food for a week but there was no way I could carry it back up the hill. I waited for two and a half hours for a lift, sheltering from a heavy rainfall in a sawmill. Eventually I got a lift from a British expatriate. In the late afternoon there was knock on the door and two British travellers, Gary and Sandy, walked in. We had previously met at the Cairo Youth Hostel and I was pleased to have company.

Other than a day when I felt ill, I spent the days walking in the hills, sometimes with Sandy and Gary, other times on my own, getting my strength back. One afternoon we went to see a neighbour of the guest house, a friendly and generous Turkish man called Mustafa who ran a potato farm.

'Welcome to my home,' said Mustafa, standing in the doorway of his house wearing an apron. 'I'm busy cooking dinner.' He was clearly used to visitors. He cooked us a beautiful meal and we had a conversation long into the night, drinking his whisky. 'I have lived here many years hidden away from the fighting,' he said. 'I have a lot of respect for the Sudanese people of the south and do my best to create work and a good livelihood for the people who work on my farm.'

The next day we went back to meet Mustafa and together we walked up a nearby hill, meeting masses of monkeys. I saw one close up for the first time. It was very small, with white hair on its back, a black head and a long black tail with a white tip.

After that we walked to a beautiful waterfall on the Kinyeti River. There was a small pool at the base with two rocky waterfalls below where we swam. Above were trees, ferns and many tropical plants. It was a real paradise. There were clouds of butterflies of many colours: dark green, purple, orange and more. We returned to the potato farm where Mustafa fed us a late lunch.

There was an excellent selection of maps and guidebooks at the guest house and I spent some time planning the rest of my journey. I would return to Juba, travel to Uganda and then Kenya, heading for Lamu on the Indian Ocean coast. I then planned to travel back to Uganda, then to Zaire (now Democratic Republic of Congo) and south to Zambia, Zimbabwe, South Africa and finally Swaziland.

After eight days I felt ready to move on and I had only two days left on my visa. I had slept well, eaten well and exercised, and was mentally in a good place. I said goodbye to Sandy and Gary, walked down the hill and took the bus back to Juba, spending the night in a local police station – an option that was always on offer for free, if you were happy to sleep behind bars. I felt sad to leave Gilo and had learned that I should break my travelling to stay at restful places when I came across them.

The next morning I waited three hours for the bus to Nimule, the border town with Uganda. By the time the bus departed it was the middle of the day and incredibly hot. Twenty miles out of Juba the bus got a flat tyre and all of us passengers had to disembark. Fortunately, most vehicles carried spare tyres and other parts, as well as jacks to lift the wheel and all kinds of tools to deal with any eventuality. When we set off again we passed through intense green hills and simple, neat villages, stopping for *shi* at a Ugandan refugee village.

The bus arrived in Nimule in the late afternoon. Today the town is the most economically important in the country, entry point for many of Uganda's exports to South Sudan. In the late 1970s it had been the entry point for refugees fleeing the terror in Uganda, inflicted by Idi Amin, whose dictatorship had come to an end a year before I arrived. I would learn more about this soon.

I spent my final night in Sudan staying in the police station and customs post on the Sudanese side of the border. I slept on the veranda of the building with my mosquito net strung up, falling asleep watching an electric lightning storm streak light across the sky and light up parts of the distant hills. A great way to end my time in the country.

3

UGANDA

GAME PARK

As the sun rose, I went to the border office for my final Sudanese stamp in my passport before hitching a lift on the back of a lorry, along with seven travellers of various nationalities. The next stop was Atiak and the Ugandan border post. Here the customs officials were very relaxed, with not even a stamp in my passport. I had a good milky tea with the border guards before we drove on to Gulu.

Although the people looked very similar to those I'd met in the south of Sudan, the difference in the two countries was noticeable. The land was on a plateau, more fertile and with much more agriculture. Many people worked the land, harvesting onions, cucumbers, carrots, tomatoes, okra, peppers and lettuce as well as vegetables new to me. These included the tangy green vegetable *malakwang*, a local delicacy; *amaranthus doodo*, a high-yielding, fast-growing leafy vegetable; *sukumawiki*, the local kale; and African spider flower, which although considered a weed, grew on the side of roads and was edible. There was fruit everywhere: mangoes, papaya, bananas, citrus, pineapples and more. Today Uganda is the top fruit-producing nation in Central Africa.

Despite the abundance of crops, Uganda was shockingly poor. I went into a few shops to look for food and found nothing. In one, the shelves around the walls were empty other than four tins of condensed milk. I couldn't understand how shopkeepers could make a living.

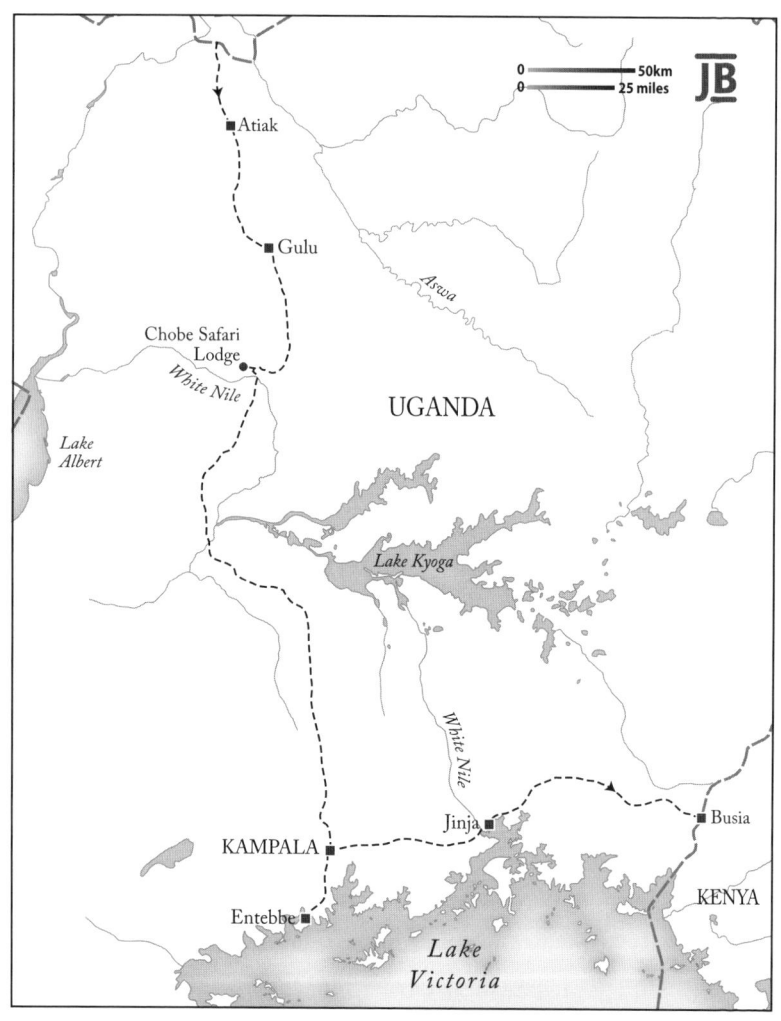

I then had to undertake a complicated black market currency transaction, turning US dollars into Ugandan shillings via Kenyan shillings. This was when I discovered that the Ugandan economy had crashed. The black market exchange rate had become the effective exchange rate at 10 times the official exchange rate. No one in their right mind traded at the official exchange rate except the government services such as post, telephones and government-owned hotels, as I soon found out. The economy had taken control of itself, which had caused a lot of poverty, especially for people who worked for the government.

I heard that there was a government lodge in the national park at Chobe, about 90 miles from Gulu. This was on the banks of the Nile and would be charged at the government exchange rate, making it by far the cheapest and most luxurious accommodation I would stay at throughout the whole journey. More importantly it would offer the chance to see some wildlife.

With other travellers I waited three hours for a lift until a bus came and dropped us at the junction of the main road and the 10-mile track to Chobe. By now it was dark, so we slept by the side of the road, each of us keeping watch for two hours at a time. In the morning some kind people from a nearby village brought us a meal of beans and rice. We waited until midday, occasionally chatting to and sharing cigarettes with soldiers guarding the entrance to the park. Just after midday a lorry stopped and we climbed on to the back. As we drove up I saw what was once a smart hotel with a block of bedrooms overlooking the River Nile. The food was European and there was cold bottled beer at the bar. The rooms were modern and clean, with en-suite bathrooms, the only time on the whole journey that I had this luxury. I shared a room with Cor from Canada, and we spent the afternoon on our balcony watching hippos bathing in the Nile below.

I woke the next morning to an incredible sunrise which I could see from the balcony, looking down on the hippos again. After a breakfast of grapefruit juice, pineapple, fried eggs and coffee, Cor and I walked up the bank of the Nile seeing monkeys, hawks, geese, vultures, wild pigs, baboons, storks and more hippos. We were told to keep an eye out for elephants and keep a safe distance, but we didn't see any.

Chobe Safari Lodge was originally constructed in the 1950s and had been one of Africa's most exclusive tourism destinations. Like so much in Uganda, it had suffered from the demise of the tourism industry during the time of Idi Amin's leadership. He had been deposed in April 1979 but the government was still unstable. Most of the residents were Ugandan Army soldiers, who were clearly not paying to stay there, and the only Western visitors were backpacker travellers like me, who could afford to stay because the hotel was desperate for income and charging government rates. The soldiers mostly sat about in the lobby and bar, with their rifles leaning on chairs and the counter, ignoring us travellers. I occasionally overheard snippets of their conversations and it was clear that they were very anxious about what they should do next. There was something going on.

After the soldiers had left for the night, Cor and I sat in the bar with the five other guests, all of us backpackers. We discussed the situation. On the one hand none of us had imagined that on our tight budgets we would be able to stay somewhere so luxurious with such proximity to wildlife, the reason so many tourists visited Africa. On the other there was tension with the soldiers feeling anxious about the political situation. We decided to see how things were the next evening.

Next morning the hotel staff offered us a minibus ride around the park. We all said yes and were driven around for about five hours. We saw a lot of Ugandan *kob*, a type of deer with curved horns peculiar to this park. We saw a lioness near a herd of deer, wild boar, buffalo, waterbuck, lots of monkeys and more. On the way back we drove close to the River Nile and saw more hippos again. It was a stunning tour and very generous of the staff.

When we got back the soldiers had all left. We had another discussion and as a result Jeff and Edward, both from Britain, and I decided to leave Chobe the next morning. We set off early to avoid the heat, walking the 10 miles from the lodge to the gate. Fortunately the park van appeared and took us to the entrance. We then walked down to the Karuma Falls close to the main road south. There had been a lot of heavy rain recently so enormous quantities of water were rushing down the falls at high speed. The force of the breakers on the rocks was like a massive ocean swell.

We then hitched a ride on a tractor and trailer to a nearby village where we drank coffee and ate pineapple. Almost immediately my guts started aching badly. We hitched another short ride – about 27 miles – on a truck to Kyaisimba, from where a policeman took us to Masindi, but he asked us for a lot of money once we were on the road. It was a tricky negotiation but in the end he drove us the 33 miles to Masindi for a reasonable cost. I made a mental note to avoid getting lifts from policemen. I'd been lulled by the hospitality of the Sudanese police. I was in a lot of pain, so we found a hostel and I spent the next hour in the toilet. The colour of my liquid suggested dysentery or food poisoning and I hoped it was only the latter.

MILITARY COUP

I woke up feeling better, if pretty weak, and decided to continue travelling with Jeff and Edward. This felt preferable to travelling on my own as I was feeling vulnerable. We got a local *matatu* up to the main road and then waited for a ride to Kampala, a distance of 130 miles. *Matatu* are privately owned minibuses used as shared taxis in Kenya and Uganda and were the main and often the only form of public transport.

Lorries and cars passed us by and for a couple of hours we didn't get a ride. We were beginning to discuss alternatives when what looked like a large military lorry with a khaki canvas cover started to slow down, and sure enough it stopped. They asked whether we would like a lift to Kampala. We looked at each other and said 'Yes please', and next thing we and our small backpacks were in the back with a group of Ugandan soldiers. They all had rifles and there were a couple of large machine guns. They were listening intently to a crackly radio. It wasn't music they were listening to, but the news.

I already knew that the dictator Idi Amin had fled the country a year ago. He had attempted to invade neighbouring Tanzania, whose army fought back, invading Uganda. There was still political instability with Godfrey Binaisa being the second president in a year. There were Tanzanian troops on the ground in Uganda and particularly in Kampala, the capital. The news on the radio was that Binaisa had been overthrown by a military coup four days ago. The soldiers were discussing the situation, mostly speaking English albeit in a local dialect. We started hearing comments such as, 'Which side are we on?', 'Should we carry on to Kampala?' and 'Who will pay our wages?'

They were scared. Yes they had guns and they clearly had orders to drive to Kampala, but these were young men, my age and in many cases younger. Of course they were scared and so was I.

Edward, Jeff and I started discussing what we should do, but the lorry was charging ahead on the bumpy road at a fair pace and we could hardly jump off. I worried that one of the guns would go off by accident.

It took over five hours to get to Kampala. We stopped at a couple of military roadblocks and our travel companions chatted to the soldiers there. My sense was that these conversations were reassuring. We were entering the western outskirts of Kampala when the lorry came to a stop. One of the drivers came to the back. 'It would be safer for you to get out now and find somewhere to stay before darkness,' he said. 'There is a curfew and everyone must to be indoors by six pm.' We had one hour.

Asking around at the lorry park we were directed to the Catholic Social Club in the suburb of Mengo. We found a *matatu* heading that way and jumped in. Thankfully the Catholic Social Club had rooms available and in no time I had a very clean and cheap room to myself. They even offered us dinner, which to my delight was vegetarian. Over dinner we heard more about the coup. Last Friday President Binaisa had dismissed the Army Chief of Staff. On Saturday the troops cut off all communications, occupied the Post Office, radio station and a hotel where for some reason all the members of Parliament were staying. Yesterday a new military-led government had been announced, along with the 6pm to 6am curfew, policed by a combination of Ugandan and Tanzanian soldiers.

James, another traveller staying at the Social Club, joined Jeff, Edward and me for dinner. He told a tale of a Ugandan friend being shot at and other stories about the last few days. I decided to take these reports at face value despite my suspicion about the pride he appeared to take in what he perceived as his adventures.

KAMPALA

In the morning I had a chat with the staff of the Social Club. The news was that Kampala was back to normal and the only evidence of the coup was the ongoing curfew. They said I would be safe to go into the city.

I found a very full *matatu* with one space free. In the city the large market was teeming with people. It was full of the colour of fabrics and the smells of cooking food. There was a lot more food here in the city than in the north, with the best Ugandan fruit and vegetables. I was still being careful about what I was eating following the previous few days, so ate a tiny portion of beans and rice which felt good where it mattered. I went to look at the craft stalls and their array of Masai blankets in bright red checked patterns from Kenya, wooden statues of gorillas, stools, bark cloth handbags and much more. There were stalls selling drums, wooden wind instruments and *mbira*, a traditional finger-plucking instrument.

I had heard that the YWCA[9] offered a cheap and delicious lunch so I headed there and found Edward and Jeff eating. The food was fabulous and largely vegetarian including a delicious groundnut paste like the *pivinda* I'd eaten in Sudan. Later Jeff and I walked through an industrial estate to the Bata shoe factory, as the one pair of shoes I had left the UK with were starting to fall apart. We were met by a very friendly Scottish expatriate who helped us both buy strong and comfortable shoes for a tiny amount of money. He told us a bit about Bata, one of the largest shoe companies in the world, with a significant presence in Africa. We then headed back to Mengo and the Catholic Social Club well before the curfew.

---

9 ⊘ ywcavti.ac.ug

I spent the next few days in Kampala. I needed to go to the Kenyan embassy to check out the visa situation. I bought some second-hand clothes in the market as many of mine were falling apart. And as I was getting bitten by mosquitos occasionally and running low on repellent I bought a few bottles. I didn't want to contract malaria: I always slept under my mosquito net and was taking a daily dose of Maloprim, the anti-malaria pills. But being struck down by malaria was still a high risk.

I was keen to visit the Bahá'í Temple in Kampala. My grandmother was a member of the Bahá'í faith [10] and the representative of Ireland (North and South) on the World Council of Bahá'ís. Bahá'ís believe that all the major religions are working towards the same ideals. They were very involved in the founding of the United Nations and have a prayer room at the UN General Assembly in New York. For some time Uganda was home to the largest Bahá'í community in Africa.

My grandmother had visited this temple, which was a beautiful green domed building that at the time of its completion was the tallest building in East Africa. Idi Amin had banned the Bahá'í faith and although the ban had been rescinded in the previous year, the temple had been ransacked and was not yet open. I walked around the perimeter fence and found the caretaker.

'Good morning,' I said. 'My grandmother, Lisbeth Greeves, visited here some years ago.'

He was silent at first, with a quizzical look, and then smiled, saying, 'I remember Mrs Greeves, she is a lovely woman.'

He took me to his small shed and made tea for us both.

---

10   bahai.org

'Your grandmother came to visit us over ten years ago,' he said. 'It was difficult in the years under Amin and some of our leaders were murdered.'

We carried on talking for about an hour and he explained how difficult the last few years had been, with Baháʼís facing repression and persecution and the religion having been banned in many countries. Yet the caretaker who had lived through all this was a very positive man, looking forward. When I left I thanked him and we shook hands for a long time. I gave him one of my London postcards, wishing I had a picture of my gran to give him too.

Every day I was in Kampala I tried to phone home. This involved a long queue at the Post Office. It was worth it because as a government service it was 10 times cheaper than it would have been if applying black market exchange rates. I wanted to speak to my parents and sisters but each time I called the phone rang but no one answered. This was in the days before voicemail messages and missed call information, so they would not know that I had called them. Each time I tried and failed I felt sad, missing them. I was really frustrated as Kampala was one of the few cities where I could afford to make a phone call home. I wrote letters to them all and sent them from the Post Office. I bought some batik for my sisters and posted these. I ate most days at the YWCA which is still operating today. On my last day I went to Entebbe and sat on the shore of Lake Victoria in the botanical gardens. I looked out at a few islands and on to the endless horizon of water, more of a sea than a lake.

After five days in Kampala, I was ready to move on and got a ride in a *matatu* to Jinja, passing over the Owen Falls dam, which has an incredible drop of 102 feet. I arrived in the afternoon after a three-hour journey. Jinja was the industrial centre of Uganda. Many of the houses were the smartest I had seen, although there were plenty of derelict properties too, evidence of the warfare and oppression of the recent years. There were very few beggars and, as far as I could see, almost everyone was working, many of them as gardeners at the larger properties. There were some Sikh and Hindu temples but most had been damaged, largely due to the anti-Asian feeling whipped up by Idi Amin from 1971. [11]

I booked into the YMCA, sleeping on the floor of a classroom. Eating a simple dinner in an Asian café where a local band played African and Asian music, I got into conversation about music with a couple of local guys of around my age. They hadn't heard much about the music I liked at home, although they were familiar with the Rolling Stones. 'Where will I hear the best music in Africa?' I rather cheekily asked them, expecting them to say Uganda, where the music was great. They both immediately answered: 'Zaire.'

The next day I stood beneath the railway bridge over the river where the White Nile leaves Lake Victoria and starts its journey to the Mediterranean Sea. I had mostly followed its path since I had arrived in Egypt. I sat for a while and remembered meeting the Nile at Cairo and following it through Egypt, down the length of Sudan and eventually to this point.

[11]   ⌀ youtube.com/watch?v=CZEvHUns9oM

4

KENYA AND UGANDA AGAIN

KENYA

TRAINS AND *MATATU*

Around mid-morning I walked across the border from Uganda to Kenya. Often two different countries are pretty similar on either side of their border. Not here. I had left Jinja early in the morning, taking the bus to Busia. It's a town of two halves: Busia Uganda and Busia Kenya. The border was in the middle. The two halves were very different as Uganda was so poor, and in 1980 the road through Busia Uganda was a dirt track with just a few stalls selling very little.

At the border post the officials took a cursory glance at my passport, stamped it and waved me on. It was a short walk on the road to the Kenyan border post. They seemed very relaxed, had a look at my passport, stamped it and waved me through. On the Kenyan side I stopped in a nice café where I drank a cold beer and listened to a band playing great music.

The people looked and sounded the same but it was instantly visible that this was a wealthier country than anywhere I had been since Israel. I walked into a few shops and the shelves were full of items that I hadn't seen for a while, chocolate being the most exciting. But the downside was the cost. Everything was more expensive than I had previously encountered, especially food, transport and accommodation. I'd have to tighten my belt if I wanted to stay in Kenya for a while, which I did.

I had heard that hitching was difficult in Kenya so took a *matatu* ride to Kisumu which stopped at every tiny village for people to get on and off. I chatted with the passengers. 'What are you doing here?' I was asked. I explained my journey. 'What's your favourite country?'

'Kenya, of course,' I replied.

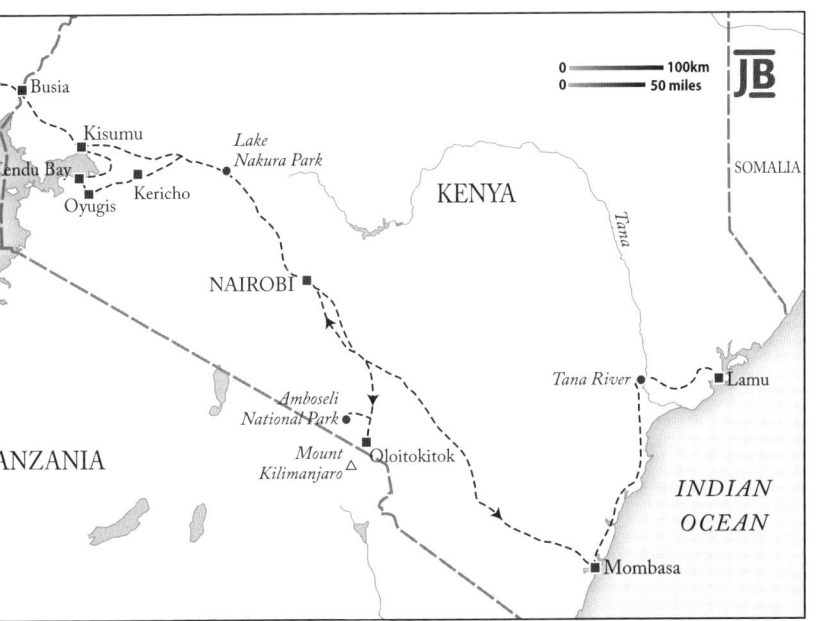

They laughed. They wanted to know what I was doing and why I was travelling. I was asked masses of questions about the places I had travelled through so far. I really enjoyed these conversations.

At Kisumu I headed to the YWCA. The town was the most affluent I had experienced so far, with plenty of shops, bars, places to eat and hotels. But the reason I wanted to come here was for the steam engines. I had learned that there was a yard where East African Railways kept their engines, and I was keen to see them. I was a railway geek as a child and still am.

I asked around and was soon walking to what was once the terminus of the train line on Lake Victoria. This was a yard with many buildings, rail tracks and, most importantly, five steam engines. They were magnificent and in extremely good condition. I wandered through the open gate and was walking around marvelling at these great steam engines when I heard a loud noise. One of the engines was being started up. I followed the sound around the side of a shed to find a beautiful green engine with a driver high up in the cab. I waved at him and he gestured for me to come over.

Of course I did and I climbed up to join him in the cab. We could not really talk because of the noise. He gestured at me to stand by his side while he shifted the gearstick and the engine slowly started to move a short distance down the track. It came to a slow halt and he applied the brake handle. There was steam everywhere and my clothes were covered in coal dust, but I didn't mind. I had always harboured a childhood fantasy about driving a steam engine and here I was. It was thrilling.

When the driver closed down the engine everything went quiet. 'Welcome to Eastern African Railways,' he said. 'I'm Okeyo and I've been driving these steam engines since I was a young man.

And what are you doing here?' he asked in a warm manner. He had spotted a fellow railway enthusiast.

'I have always loved steam trains,' I replied. 'And I have travelled overland all the way from Egypt to come and see these.' He laughed.

I told Okeyo about childhood visits to the Ffestiniog Railway in North Wales and the Bluebell Railway in East Sussex. We chatted for a while and then climbed down from the cab and he gave me a tour. There were a number of really beautiful engines and Okeyo told me about how his job was to keep them in good condition for when they might be needed again. My sense was that this might never happen and he probably knew that, but his pride in keeping these engines in such good condition shone through. It was dark by the time I left. I thanked him and gave him one of my postcards. We shook hands and I headed back to the YWCA.

The next day I wanted to take a ferry ride on Lake Victoria so I could best see some of this enormous lake. After waiting an hour there was a ferry to Kendu Bay. It was a beautiful ride in a boat the size of a London Thames tour boat. The lake is enormous – more of a sea. As always I got into a great conversation with a man who decided he would be my tour guide for the trip and told me all about the lake and pointed out the fishing boats, explaining what they were catching. After two hours we arrived at Kendu Bay, where after a short break for tea I went to the nearby *matatu* stand. I wanted to see if there was a *matatu* all the way to Kericho, but that wasn't an option.

I found asking for help with transport or anything else was easy. Everyone was really helpful and accurate, except sometimes where there was a potential sale involved. I was learning to distinguish between the two. I climbed into a packed *matatu* to the small town of Oyugis, which took about 45 minutes as it didn't stop much. I was again grateful for the fact that I was carrying such a small backpack, with my tent and sleeping bag tied on to the bottom, as these had to sit on my knee. Everyone had to carry their luggage – often chickens and other animals – on their knees. Arriving at Oyugis all the passengers got out and immediately climbed into another *matatu* heading to Kisii. Just as well I moved quickly as otherwise I wouldn't have got on myself.

Matatus were brightly decorated with images of famous people or places, to attract customers. They would pick up passengers anywhere they were flagged down on their main route and drop people off at any point, sometimes going miles off the route to drop people at their home for an extra payment. This was very annoying for the other passengers as it extended the length of their journey, with no discount offered. *Matatus* were technically regulated in Kenya by 1980 but it seemed to me that there was little in the way of enforcement. They broke down regularly, burst tyres being a frequent occurrence. Seat belts were rarely installed and speeding was pretty much par for the course. On the plus side, this was the cheapest way of travelling. Hitchhiking appeared to be frowned upon in Kenya and I had not seen any hitchhikers of any race on the roads since I'd arrived. More importantly I was travelling the way that most Kenyans travelled, so I had plenty of great conversations and learned a lot about people's lives and opinions. 'I am so sorry you had to travel in Uganda, not a happy country,' said one woman.

When we arrived in Kisii it was 2pm and still a fair way to Kericho. I thought about staying the night. But I didn't and it was a mistake. I found a *matatu* going the rest of the way to Kericho. It took five hours to cover the 55 miles. The engine kept packing in and each stop took ages. The worst was when it took half an hour to get four passengers off and another four on with all their baggage in tow. Five hours sitting in a fully loaded *matatu* was uncomfortable and when we drew up in Kericho at sunset I had a bad case of 'traveller's arse'.

If I focused on the beautiful view I felt better. The hills were covered with small family-owned fields known as *shambas*. This was an example of the agroforestry system practised in East Africa, where various crops were combined: bananas, beans, yams and corn, alongside timber resources, beekeeping, medicinal herbs, mushrooms, forest fruits and fodder for livestock. They made very good use of the land here, which could account for the higher standard of living I observed compared with Uganda and Sudan.

When we finally arrived in Kericho a very friendly policeman directed me to a cheap, clean hostel. I ate a simple meal of beans, vegetables and rice in a little café nearby and slept well, recovering from my aches.

WILDLIFE

I left Kericho in the morning. I preferred to be in the countryside, which was endlessly fascinating, and hoped to visit Lake Nakura Park without spending money on a tourist package. The drive passed through beautifully ordered tea plantations for most of the 75 miles. On arrival I bought food at the market and walked down to the lake, pitching my tent on a piece of hidden wasteland close to the road. There was heavy rain in the night which woke me, but I stayed dry in the tent.

In the morning I packed up my tent and sat waiting for a lift. I was keen to go into the park. As I waited I was befriended by a baboon who tried to pick my pockets. I wasn't having this and so eventually he settled down, sitting a little way away from me but keeping an eye in case I dropped my guard. Around mid-morning a busload of people drew up and stopped. They explained that they were on a forestry seminar and that they were spending the afternoon visiting the park. They offered for me to join them, which was what I had hoped for. There were Kenyans, Tanzanians, Zambians, Nigerians, Finns and Mauritians. They were waved through into the park and so I got a free entry too. The bus drove around the lake, past pink flamingos, pelicans and cormorants. We were driven to the top of a cliff where a buffet lunch was laid out in a lookout café. I devoured a huge plate as I hadn't eaten much over the last day and a half. After lunch the bus drove on and we saw colobus monkeys, various types of deer and waterbuck, buffaloes, baboons, wild boars and giraffes. They dropped me off just outside the entrance to the park and I pitched the tent for the night. It was a brilliant day.

I walked into Nakuru the next morning and caught a bus to Nairobi. Arriving was a bit of culture shock. Nairobi was very Western, with skyscrapers, banks, chain stores and even a Woolworths. The traffic congestion was the worst I had ever seen, this at a time when the Nairobi metropolitan region had a population of 862,000. In 2023 it was estimated at 5,325,000[12].

MALARIA

I found a shared room for a reasonable cost at New Kenya Lodge on River Road, a popular road for travellers in the centre. I woke in

---

12   macrotrends.net/cities/21711/nairobi/population#:~:text=The%20current %20metro%20area%20population,a%203.95%25%20increase%20from%20 2020

the middle of the night absolutely soaked in sweat. I had a crashing headache. I felt nauseous. I lay in the bed trying not to worry but something wasn't right. At first I convinced myself that it was just too hot in the room. But it didn't really feel like that. I slept fitfully and as soon as it was early enough I staggered downstairs to find the hotel manager. I told him how I was feeling.

'You have malaria,' he said.

He then told me to go to the hospital which I could get to in a *matatu*, although he suggested that if I felt I could walk the 40 minutes I would probably get there more quickly, such was the congestion. I decided to give it a try and made it to the hospital on foot. The very large lobby was full of people. I went to the reception desk and after a short wait in a queue I told them I thought I had malaria. I was immediately sent up a corridor to another desk. This was much quieter, with a sign saying 'Malaria Clinic'. A very helpful nurse asked what my symptoms were and confirmed that I had malaria. She took me to a small room and a few minutes later returned with a tray. She proceeded to give me an injection, handed me some medication and explained that I needed to get as much rest as possible. She then asked me where I was staying and how I got to the hospital. When I told her that I had walked for about 40 minutes, she was horrified.

'You're not walking back,' she commanded. 'I'll find you some transport.'

She disappeared and about 15 minutes later reappeared with a man who was going to drive me back to the hotel.

'How much should I pay?' I asked.

'Nothing,' she said. 'The hospital is free and the driver is a hospital driver.'

I have visited hospitals in the UK when I have had to wait for hours, and on one occasion overnight, to get seen by a nurse or doctor. This was perhaps the most efficient hospital visit I've ever experienced. Somehow the traffic had eased and I was back at the hotel in 25 minutes. Meanwhile Emojey the hotel manager had moved me into a single room with a ceiling fan set on the highest speed. He laid on lots of bottles of cold water. I fell into the bed and thankfully slept for a long time. I can't remember much of the next days. I drifted in and out of sleep. I had strange hallucinogenic dreams. I lost all sense of time and had a vague memory of Emojey coming in a few times to check on me. But by the third day the fever was passing and I had stopped sweating. The headache was easing. I was very weak and hadn't eaten for days, but didn't yet feel like food.

I was still very tired but ready to get up and move on. I found the city stressful, the noise, the traffic and the pollution. I wanted to get to Lamu and hopefully meet Rob, the British traveller I had met in Juba. After a light breakfast at a café on River Road, I walked over to the train station and bought a ticket for the overnight train to Mombasa. I thought of Okeyo at Kisumu, who had probably driven this train back in the days of steam. That afternoon I went to the cinema as it was the coolest place in the city, with air conditioning. I sat and watched some banal disaster movie, but it was probably a good idea to relax in the comfortable atmosphere and I must have slept through part of it.

THE COAST

I boarded the train at Nairobi Station in the early evening. I said goodbye to Emojey with lots of thanks for his helping me when I was ill. I gave him one of my postcards as my rather small thank you. Such kindness.

I sat in the buffet car of the train for the overnight journey. It was a backpacker ruse to buy a single drink and then spend the night trying to sleep on the comfy chairs. That's what I did and managed to doze a bit during the journey. This was the cheapest way to travel on the train otherwise I would have had to book a seat, or worse, a bed.

I arrived in Mombasa and found a cheap bedroom at the Hydro, a sleepy backpackers' hotel with a lot of charm. I dumped my bag and headed into town. In 1980 Mombasa was the second largest city in Kenya, with a population of 350,000. Located on the Indian Ocean, it was called the 'blue and white' town, with many blue and white painted buildings in the old part of the city. I walked to Fort Jesus, the old fortress at the entrance of the original harbour. It was built by the Portuguese in the 1580s and then captured by Arab traders a century later. I sat looking out to sea taking in a view of the turquoise ocean stretching into the horizon and dotted with small fishing boats.

The next morning I went to the bus station. I'd been told there was a bus to Lamu that left around 7am, so was there before 6.30am. Sure enough the bus was loading up with people and baggage. I met Arthur from the Netherlands and we managed to get seats.

For four hours the bus drove up the coast, coming to the first ferry just to the south of the town of Malindi. This was a pontoon ferry with an engine and the bus drove on and was taken across the river. We got out and stood on the deck of the pontoon and looked at the mangrove swamp on both banks of the river. The mangroves were extraordinary, forests of knotted trees emerging from the swampland up the coastline for miles and miles.

The bus carried on to Malindi and then went inland in the direction of Garsen. This involved crossing the Tana River on the ferry known as Ferry ya Mkono. This is long gone, as a bridge has now been built, but was still operational in 1980. It was a small pontoon not much longer or wider than the bus with a large rope stretched across the river. The bus drove on to the ferry and everyone got out. The ferry had one boatman, but all the men on the bus were expected to join in. We all stood on one side of the pontoon and tugged on the rope, pulling the pontoon complete with bus and passengers across the river.

The people here were dressed very colourfully and many women were walking along the road, carrying crops and goods on their heads or pulling small carts, often with a baby tied on to their back with fabric. The men rarely carried anything. These were the original Swahili people, part Arabic and part African. There were many animals on the road, cows and goats, and fishermen fishing in the swamp by the roadside. Eventually, after about a nine-hour drive from Mombasa, we arrived at a small jetty in the dark with some lights in the distance. After about 15 minutes a small passenger boat arrived and took us on the short, but wet, crossing to Lamu, arriving at a jetty built on to the stone harbour wall. Arthur had the address of a backpacker hostel and we checked in there. It was a beautiful old building behind the old jailhouse, with wooden doors and windows. Even by night the town was magical.

LAUNCHING THE *DHOW*

Lamu was really beautiful with small, narrow streets and white houses packed close to one another with open shutters on the small windows. The wooden doors were large, often with ornate designs, and opened right on to the streets. We headed for the harbour as our previous day's bus driver had mentioned that a *dhow* was being launched. I did not appreciate that this would be such a huge event. I thought *dhows* were small sailing boats. I could not have been more wrong.

It looked like the whole town was there. There were people everywhere. On top of one of the many piers was an enormous wooden boat, more like a small ship. It was on a wooden slipway that seemed to be quite high above the water level and I only hoped that the tide would be rising soon to meet it.

There were about twelve thick ropes tied at various points on to the *dhow*, held out in the water by men, some of whom had water up to their knees and others up to their chests. On the shoreline were hundreds of women in colourful costume singing, and on an old tower by the harbour were *mullahs*, dressed in white, saying prayers for the *dhow*. There was a reasonable number of Western travellers and it wasn't too long before I met Rob, who I had last seen in Juba. He was with Steve, who was briefly at Moshav Tomer with me.

'Welcome to Lamu,' said Rob, followed by, 'How come it took you so long?'

'That's a long story. I'll fill you in after this,' I replied.

Almost immediately men started moving among the crowd asking for help to pull on the ropes. Luckily I was wearing a pair of swimming shorts, a T-shirt and a lungi, a Swahili version of a sarong.

We immediately volunteered and were soon in the rows of men waiting to pull on the ropes to get the *dhow* into the water. There must have been around 20 men on each rope, so about 240 men in the water. The tide was rising and as Lamu has a tidal range between three and ten feet there was little time to pull the *dhow* in before all the men, including us, would have to abandon the ropes and swim for the shore.

'Why are we waiting to pull?' I asked the man next to me.

He replied, 'We must wait for the *mullahs* to complete their prayers for the safety of the *dhow* and pick the auspicious moment for launching.'

The water was above my knees and I prayed that that moment would come soon. Maybe my prayer was heard because suddenly there was the loud sound of a horn, the signal for us to pull on the ropes. The *dhow* did not move. The horn blew again and again we all pulled. Nothing. No movement. We tried to get the *dhow* moving again and again. By now the water was up to my waist and there was no sign of any movement. This carried on for another 20 minutes or so, by which time the water was rising up my chest and men on the ropes further out to sea had abandoned their posts.

The launch had failed. There was much wailing by the women and everyone let go of their ropes and swam back to shore. Once back on land there were many heated discussions. I asked a couple of the men who I had shared a rope with and they said things ranging from 'We will try again tomorrow' to 'Very inauspicious'. It was past midday by now and time for a break. It had been a superb experience, one I would never forget. What a way to arrive.

There was a feast with food laid on, and we *mzungu* who had been part of the abortive launch were invited to join. It was mostly fish which I didn't eat, but there were my old favourite beans and rice and other delicious vegetable and fruit dishes.

Mzungu? This word is used widely in East and Central Africa to refer to foreigners, and in particular white Westerners. It is a Bantu word that means 'wanderer' and was originally used to describe spirits. I had heard the word occasionally in Uganda but in Kenya it was widely used. It wasn't a derogatory term, it was simply a statement of fact. I embraced it, glad of a word to describe myself.

That afternoon Rob came to where I was staying and took me for a guided tour of Lamu Old Town. He had been in town for two weeks. We visited food shops and restaurants which he gave his reviews of, as well as some of the old buildings including the Lamu Museum, housed in an old Swahili warehouse, and Lamu Fort.

I had not heard of Lamu before I started this journey. As I learned more about the island town, it sounded like a fabled, mystical place. But nothing had prepared me for one of the most unique destinations I have ever visited. Lamu was founded in the 1300s and looked like it had not changed much in the intervening centuries. The streets were narrow, too small for cars, so carts and donkeys were used to move goods around. The buildings, predominantly white, were built from coral stone and mangrove timbers, often with elaborately carved doorways opening on to the streets. The people wore colourful clothing, contrasting with the white houses and blue sea that could be seen at the end of most of the streets. I instantly fell in love with the place.

'Come and see where I'm staying?' asked Rob after we had walked around for a while. He and Steve each had small rooms on the second floor of an old house where they could climb the stairs to get out on to the flat roof, where there was a tiny thatched shack. 'I think this is being vacated – why don't you speak to the owner about renting it?' said Rob. I jumped at the chance, spoke with the landlord and agreed I would move in the next day.

That evening our small group went to a large, beautiful house outside town occupied by a group of German women. They had a tradition of cooking food for groups of *mzungu* travellers once a week, and we all made a small contribution. The food was vegetarian and delicious and the company was wonderful. Their house was on the way to the beach and they told me to come by any time en route to or from the beach. That night I dreamed that I lived there for the rest of my life, a dream that still occasionally reoccurs.

ISLAND HEAVEN

The next day I moved into the shack on the roof above Steve and Rob. I had a single mattress on the floor with a rug and my own sheet bag. There were hooks to hang my mosquito net. There was a table with a chair and some cushions. That was it. I had shared use of the very basic bathroom on the floor below. Ocean breezes blew in through the stable door, keeping me cool and largely free of mosquitos. There was an open window with no glass or shutters and a thatched roof, which I suspected let in the rain. I loved it.

The stable door overlooked the town, looking out to the waterfront and the old jail and beyond. From the open window I could look down on the labyrinth of small streets and thatched roofs. It had been a while since I'd been able to wash my clothes, which quickly dried on the washing lines on the roof. That first evening it rained heavily and, as I had suspected, the roof leaked and I had a minor flood. The next morning the sun was out again. I unsuccessfully attempted to repair the roof but the landlord agreed to get someone up to fix it. The next morning I walked across the island to the beach, seven miles of sand with surf and scrubland in the dunes that gave a tiny bit of shade – although not enough as my nose was burnt a bit. I swam and bodysurfed in the Indian Ocean waves. I felt the best I had in a long time.

A few days quickly become a week. The call to prayer of the *mullahs* punctuated each day. I loved walking in the old town, exploring every street and ending up in quite a few dead ends, sometimes chased away by dogs. I walked the 45 minutes to the beach every day. Sometimes Rob or one of the others joined me but often I went on my own, although there were always other people swimming. I often stopped on the way back at the German women's house for a drink and a chat.

One evening there was a wedding. There were a lot of men and boys dressed in white praying on mats out in the streets to the music of flutes and drums. Then a large group of women walked through the town dressed in black and swaying to the sounds of drums and a trumpet playing a type of traditional jazz. The procession led up to a square where another band played with four drummers, cymbals (baking trays), a cornet and a flute. In the middle of the square the men were having mock fights with sticks while the women swayed, this time to a slow trumpet. A very beautiful ritual and a privilege to see.

I had been in Lamu 10 days when Rob, Wim and Eric (from the Netherlands) and I took a *dhow* trip from Shela Beach to Manda Island across the water. We took our mosquito nets, food and cooking pots. The island was pretty much deserted and we walked along 'elephant paths', although with no sign of elephants. Eventually we arrived at the ruins of a town called Takwa which was abandoned some time around the 18th century. We found a beautiful beach nearby where we hung our mosquito nets from trees. We spent two days and nights there swimming, walking and sitting around. We cooked simple stews and made *chapatis* on a wood fire. It was magical – although as four young men we did occasionally get irritated with each other.

On our last day on Manda we walked back along the beach. My Greek sandals that had got me this far finally gave up on me so I had to walk back barefoot, trying not to burn the soles of my feet in the sand. Exhausted, we finally reached the one smart hotel on the island where the staff took pity on us and gave us a meal and a boat ride back to Lamu Town. They were really kind. That evening I sat on the roof outside my shack watching the sun set. The *dhows* were sailing home and the palms were blowing in the wind. I have always missed Lamu and still would like to go back one day. It hasn't happened yet.

Lamu hasn't always been the idyllic island that I found. In September 2011, a British couple on a sailing holiday were kidnapped from a hotel by Al-Shabaab, a terrorist group based in Somalia. Three weeks later, a French woman was taken by the group from a different hotel. These and other kidnappings along the Kenyan border with Somalia resulted in an invasion of Somalia by the Kenyan army. In June 2014, armed men attacked Mpeketoni, a town on the mainland close to Lamu. They burned buildings and attacked people, killing 47 in one night. This carried on and within one month Lamu had witnessed over 100 killings, which Al-Shabaab claimed responsibility for. Needless to say travellers and tourists stopped going there.

Following these attacks, Lamu became the location of counter-terrorism activity supported by Western nations as part of the post-9/11 so-called 'War on Terror'. Security is much tighter today and the UK's Foreign Office still advises against all but essential travel in Lamu County and the whole area north of Malindi that I travelled through, excluding Lamu and Manda islands – and it was only in 2021 that the travel advisory was lifted on those.

CHANGING PLANS

Over those days in Lamu I'd talked with Rob about his plans to travel through Zaire and across multiple countries to the Sahara Desert and then back to Europe. I'd been thinking for some time that I would like to be home by my birthday in October. I felt this strong pull to be back by then for something, I just wasn't sure what it was[13]. We discussed travelling back together, although this would mean me not going to Swaziland. If I did go there it would be much longer before I got home plus I would need to find work to replenish my limited funds.

Later that evening Rob and I were eating dinner when his former partner Angie and her young son walked into the café having just arrived in Lamu. Angie and Rob had ended their relationship in Khartoum. He was pleased to see them and I knew from conversations we'd had that he would like to get back together with her. I suspected this could mean the end of us travelling to Zaire. I was anxious about travelling across that country on my own, but I had to enter Zaire wherever I was headed as the border between Kenya and Tanzania was closed.

---

13   What I couldn't have known then was that two weeks after returning in October 1980 I would meet Paul Grassick in Bristol, create Nova Wholefoods Cooperative with him, and thus launch my career as a social entrepreneur. This is a subject of my book *Creating Social Enterprise.*

I'd been on Lamu for three weeks, the longest I had stayed in one place since Israel. It was hard to leave but I did, taking the bus back to Mombasa via Tana River and Malindi. I stayed two nights in Mombasa and decided that, from then on, I would walk or hitchhike unless it was an emergency. I had done the maths and at my current rate of spending I would run out of money well before I got back to the UK.

I set off walking from Mombasa. It was very slow. I walked about 10 miles in the heat before a lorry driver stopped and drove me for about an hour until he arrived at his destination. I thanked him and started walking again. It was hot and dusty and I was beginning to regret travelling on my own. What on earth was I doing walking up a hot and virtually empty road 6,500 miles away from home? I was trying not to feel despondent when I heard a car, which slowed down and stopped. A window wound down and a familiar face popped out, saying, 'Get into the car.'

'Rob!' I shouted. 'What are you doing here?' I got into the car. Jonathon the driver was a British expatriate driving from Mombasa to Nairobi. Rob had hitched a ride from Mombasa with him in the morning and told him that he hoped that he would see me on the road.

'I wanted Angie and I to get back together, but she was very clear that she didn't want that. I felt sad so decided to set off and see if I could find you,' said Rob.

It felt very random that despite leaving Lamu separately we had met up again, but then maybe it was just meant to happen. So we started travelling together. Jonathon seemed very pleased and we chatted away until we reached the turn-off to the Amboseli National Park where he insisted that we should both go next. We slept the night in my tiny tent by the side of the road. That evening we talked about Zaire and began to actively plan our journey there. It was exciting.

The next morning we hitched a lift with some other travellers in a Land Rover which got us near to Oloitokitok, close to the border with Tanzania and Mount Kilimanjaro. They dropped us off and we started walking. The land was flat and pretty much empty, with very little vegetation. So it was a surprise to see trees up ahead. We were almost at these trees when we saw some others were there too – a small group of giraffes. We slowed down and crept up, getting very close to the tallest. It stood there for what felt like a very long time and then gently moved away with the others following. It was a magical moment.

We carried on walking and met some Masai people. We stopped and they offered us a drink of beer. Then they asked if we would like to buy some of their jewellery. Despite my now very tight budget, I asked the price of a bracelet that was offered and after some bargaining ended up buying it. I wore it for many years.

After a night camping in a field we set off to walk up to Amboseli National Park, one of the most famous in Kenya. We thought it would be a six-mile walk but it was much longer. Eventually we walked off the road to find a park gate surrounded by Masai souvenir shops. We could not enter the park without paying a fee that was quite beyond our budgets. So we hung out with the Masai instead. Once they realised that we were not wealthy tourists, some of the men invited us back to their nearby village where we met some of their wives and children. Their village, called a *boma*, was made up of a circle of *enkaji* (houses), built with branches covered with several layers of a mixture of soil, urine and cow dung.

I liked the Masai. They seemed to have created a realistic balance between their traditional life and the modern world. They made money from selling traditional crafts, jewellery and costume but still lived in the types of houses I suspect they had lived in for centuries. Like the Dinka of Sudan, the Masai are tall, averaging over six feet. Those we met were wearing red or blue checked cotton robes, called *shuka*, wrapped over their backs or shoulders. Many of them wore sandals made of what looked like car tyres.

That night we camped in my tent on the edge of a churchyard. We woke up in the night freezing cold and put on every piece of clothing that we had, which wasn't enough. After months of hot nights as well as days, this was a shock. I regretted trading in my sleeping bag for a rug in Sudan. We woke to an incredible view of Mount Kilimanjaro and the lesser-known Mount Meru to one side.

We walked back to Amboseli and sat by the entrance for a few hours. Eventually one of the staff arrived and told us that we would be admitted into the park without having to pay. We were driven in a park Land Rover to a basic campsite on the edge of a green swampy area. It was set in dense vegetation of trees, ferns and bushes. We explored carefully and suddenly saw six large elephants tearing up grass for food. We crouched down, hiding in the vegetation as best we could, watching them move very gracefully, as if in slow motion, despite their enormous size. Eventually they saw us and bolted off.

We saw giraffes, bucks, kobs, zebra, wildebeest and more. And so many monkeys, much cheekier than the Egyptian ones. If we looked away from our food for a second it was gone. One got into our tent and quickly snuck away with the bread. Nearby were birds with beautiful blue, green and purple wings which shone in the light. All this and an incredible view of Kilimanjaro.

The next morning I woke up before Rob. It was really dark outside, which didn't make sense. I gently opened the zip door flap of the tent and just outside was a huge elephant walking right past, less than three feet away, followed by another large elephant and two younger ones of varying sizes. I crouched in the entrance of the tent, barely breathing, taking in this incredible sight. After they had passed I realised that if they had been any closer that would have been the end of us both.

Later one of the staff from the Amboseli Safari Lodge walked over to the campsite to invite us to breakfast, which was very generous of them. The Lodge was empty, which didn't make sense to us but was certainly to our advantage as we had a really huge breakfast. Then they offered us a Land Rover ride around part of the park. We saw a leopard, wild dogs, buffalo, zebra, two lions and more elephants and giraffes. It was fantastic and I couldn't quite believe that they were doing this for us. The next morning one of the Lodge staff came with the Land Rover and took us to the entrance of the park. I could not believe their generosity and all I had to give them was a couple of my postcards.

It took a couple of days to hitchhike and walk to the Ugandan border at Busia. We walked across the border after buying a couple of chocolate bars, the last we would eat for a while.

BACK TO UGANDA

CURFEW

Arriving in Kampala we went straight to the Embassy of Zaire to apply for visas. This was, as usual, slow and difficult and the staff seemed surprised that we wanted to travel to their country. Worst of all this meant leaving our passports overnight. We appeared to have no option, so after a short discussion we agreed to hand them over in exchange for a signed receipt and a promise of our visas in the morning.

We had to find accommodation and agreed that for a number of reasons we should stay in a hotel. The main reason was the overnight curfew which was still in place. Kampala was a dangerous city and we didn't want to take excessive risks. We found a room in a hotel near the Zairean Embassy and settled in for the night. The hotel room was on the fourth floor and quite small: two single beds, a small table and chair and a window looking down on the street. The fan in the ceiling was noisy, but the worst noise was the sound of gunfire on the street below. At one point, when there was a lull in the shooting, we looked out of the window. We saw three bodies lying in the street below and shut the window quickly, shaking with fear.

We were scared. We locked the door of the room but that didn't feel enough. We took the table and chair and pushed them against the door up against the handle so we would at least have some protection if someone tried to kick the door in. Realistically, though, that would only have bought us a few seconds and in any case we had no escape route. We sat down and played cards to calm down. That was fine for a while until there was a knock on the door. We froze.

After what felt like a long time, but wasn't, I said, 'Who is there?'

'Another *mzungu*,' answered a voice that sounded English.

'Can you just wait a minute?' I said, looking at Rob. He nodded at me, suggesting we should open the door. We pulled the chair and table back and opened the door. 'What are you doing here?' I asked in amazement.

'Who is this?' asked Rob, who was really confused.

'Patrick and I were at Bristol University together,' answered Guy. 'I might have known that he would be doing something as crazy as this.' He had arrived at the hotel just before the curfew and the staff had told him that there were other *mzungu* staying. He had no idea that I was travelling in Africa, let alone Uganda [14].

Guy continued, 'I'm only in Uganda for a few weeks. I'm on a legal investigation. And I just changed hotels today because mine felt too dangerous. This one seems quieter.'

'It's pretty noisy outside,' I said. The anxiety and then excitement of Guy's arrival in our room had meant Rob and I had temporarily forgotten about the shooting outside. The three of us spent the rest of the evening talking.

After a fitful night interrupted by gunfire, Rob and I returned to the Zairean Embassy. To our great relief our passports were stamped with visas to travel. I still have the passport with this and many other visas and stamps. Signed by Omary Biladi, the Deuxième Conseiller, this Zairean visa is in French, which was the official language of Zaire and many of the countries I would soon travel through. I was about to test my O-level French, for which I had only just scraped a pass.

I went to the Post Office and joined the queue for an international call. And to my great surprise I got through to speak

---

14   Guy Dehn went on to become the founding director of Public Concern at Work, the charity that was formed in 1993 and became Protect in 2018. He trained as a barrister and was one of the drivers behind the UK's whistleblowing legislation – helping to draft the Private Members' bills that eventually became the Public Interest Disclosure Act.

with Mum. It was so lovely to hear her voice. No one else was at home. I felt a little homesick when I finished the call and cheered myself up by doing some rare shopping. I really liked the sandals that I had seen the Masai wear, made out of car tyres, and went to a market where I had heard they were made. The market was around the edge of a large open space where *matatu* taxis congregated and almost immediately I saw a huge pile of old car tyres, surrounded by about 10 young men sitting on the ground cutting and stitching the rubber to make the sandals. I tried a few before choosing a pair that felt very comfortable. Little did I know how many miles I would walk in them before I got back home and that they would survive the trip intact. The best sandals I have ever had.

When I got back to the hotel mid-afternoon there was a Zairean band playing. They were fantastic, watched by a great crowd of mostly Ugandans; all those I spoke to said that Zaire had the best music in all of Africa. We were back in the room by curfew hoping that we wouldn't hear gunfire again. Sadly we did.

Guy had left Kampala and Rob and I were on our way to Zaire. We could not wait to get going, but the trains were not running for three days. Given the risk of violence we decided not to hitchhike out of the city. I was less naïve and more cautious than I had been when I took the lift into Kampala with a lorryload of uncertain soldiers during the coup.

That weekend we stayed safe. We stayed in or close to the hotel as there were bodies on the street every morning. The hotel gossip was that the Tanzanian soldiers were not being properly paid so there was extortion of people on the streets after curfew and this accounted for the bodies. I had no idea whether this was true but didn't enquire further. We spent every afternoon listening to the

Zairean band in the hotel. We asked some of the band members about what they thought it would be like for us travelling in Zaire. They said we would be fine and seemed pleased that we wanted to go. I loved the music; it was dance music with a beat but also soulful and sometimes mournful. They played guitars, drums and brass instruments with the whole band singing.

LEAVING

We booked the train from Kampala to Kasese, a town in the west of Uganda close to the border with Zaire. We left Kampala station mid-afternoon and the train arrived in Mityana station about three hours later. The carriage was surprisingly empty and it wasn't until we arrived that we understood why. The train was terminating and there would be no more services west until the next evening. We asked the staff where we could sleep and they offered us a small room off the waiting room where we hung our mosquito nets.

The next day we woke early. The station was empty, with no staff or passengers. We ventured out to a beautiful sight. The station was in the middle of jungle, with trees of all sorts, flowers of every colour and the sound of birds. There was a small track which we assumed led to a town but there was no sign of any vehicles. We had enough food for a few days, mostly dried fruit and nuts, so decided to stay where we were, enjoying a day of absolutely no travelling at all.

By late afternoon some of the station staff arrived and as darkness fell passengers started turning up. Eventually the train from Kampala drew in with the promise of an overnight journey to Kasese. And it was full. Rob and I boarded and stood for most of the night. As the sun rose, the train came to the station at the end of the line. We had eaten some food and were ready to hit the road. We got a lift from the station to Katunguru and a junction where we left the main road.

My now battered map of the roads of Africa showed that there was a road from here to the Zairean border. This was no longer tarmac, but a long, hot, dusty track. We walked for about two hours with no vehicles to be seen. By now it was a very hot mid-morning and the road was pretty inhospitable with thorns often spreading across in front of our feet. There were no animals or people to be seen. After a very hot and exhausting walk a Land Rover appeared and its two Ugandan drivers welcomed us in. We drove around the side of a hill and suddenly we could see an enormous lake, Lake Edward. On my map it was called Lake Idi Amin, its name from 1973 to 1979 before Amin was overthrown and it reverted back to its colonial name.

They drove us down to a small, very isolated fishing village on the shores of the lake where we saw enormous shark-like creatures that the fishermen had caught. After a lunch of beans at a roadside café we set off walking. It wasn't long before two large Kenyan lorries arrived heading for Zaire, driving together. They stopped and offered us a lift. I got into the driver's cab of the first and Rob the second. The road was the worst I had encountered so far, even worse than in Sudan. It was full of pot-holes in the dirt and some parts were partially washed away. It wasn't long before the larger lorry behind got stuck in a pot-hole. We all got out, the drivers brought out a chain and fastened it between the two vehicles, and the smaller lorry started to pull the larger one out. With some pushing from Rob and me we eventually got the larger lorry out. By the time we arrived at the border at Ishasha it was getting dark.

5

ZAIRE

GOMA

It was dark as we left Uganda and walked the 20 yards across to the border of Zaire. At the tiny border post we showed our passports with their elaborate, full-page visas and were welcomed by the head customs officer. It quickly became clear that we were among the very few travellers crossing this border, but extraordinarily we met two Brits, Claire and Sharon, who were about to cross to Uganda. The customs men had a short discussion between themselves and then all four of us were brought to a small dining room at the back of the building where we were served a French-style leek potage. We were then shown two empty offices where we could stay the night, one for Rob and me and one for Claire and Sharon. A very generous welcome.

The four of us chatted well into the night. 'Where have you travelled from?' asked Sharon over dinner.

I started. 'I travelled overland from Jericho to Cairo, then by train to Luxor and Aswan. The boat from Aswan to Sudan was incredible. I then took the train from Wadi Halfa to Khartoum and then had a wild trip on top of lorries to Juba where I first met Rob.'

Rob carried on. 'I travelled pretty much the same route to Juba but then went east to Lake Turkana in Kenya, then on to Lamu.'

'And I met him there after going through Uganda to Nairobi, where I was sick with malaria, before heading to Lamu.'

'That's pretty much what we plan to do in reverse,' said Claire.

'How did you get here?' asked Rob.

Sharon gave their summary. 'We went from Spain to Morocco, then Algeria and across the desert to Niger, across Nigeria to Cameroon, then Congo and down to Kinshasa, up the river to Kisangani on the ferry and then on lorries through the rainforest to here.'

'We plan to travel to Uganda and Kenya and then head north, like you both,' said Claire. 'Although we hadn't thought about Lamu. What's it like?'

'You have to go,' Rob and I both said in unison.

We plied each other with questions about the road, how best to travel, places to stay and places to see. I bought out my

notebook and wrote down lots of their tips and they did the same. Towards the end of the evening, I asked them, 'How safe have you found hitchhiking?'

Claire said, 'Like you both, we've chosen to pay for transport sometimes because it felt safer. But otherwise we've hitchhiked and felt safer doing that on this trip than in Britain.' Sharon agreed.

In the morning we said goodbye to Claire and Sharon and they headed over the border to Uganda. I never saw them again but I'm pretty confident that they made it home.

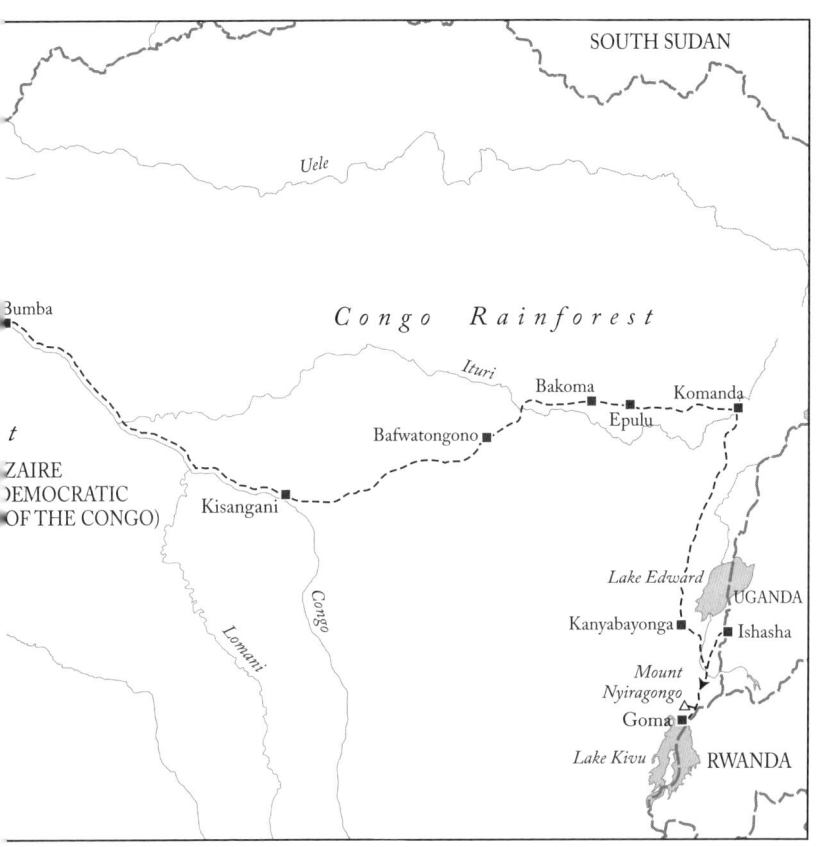

Rob and I thanked the head of the border post and I gave him one of the postcards. We started walking along the dusty road. On both sides it was very green with lots of banana plants, maize, cassava and strange red plants that looked like broccoli. There were villages all the way along the route and plenty of people walking the road. Rob spoke French very well and mine was returning, so we conversed with people as we walked. We were clearly an unusual sight, which meant lots of women, men and children came up to talk with us. This was fun.

Towards the end of the morning vehicles started appearing and it wasn't long before we got into a car with, to our surprise, the head of the border post. He stopped at the next town, Rutshuru, and we went to find something to eat in the tiny market there. After lunch we carried on walking down the road past banana trees and coffee plantations. The soil was so fertile largely because of proximity to the volcanos of the Virunga mountains. Eventually a lorry appeared that looked like it would be the perfect vehicle to take us through the foothills of the volcanos, but it soon broke down. We got out with the two other passengers and the four of us pushed it a long way down a hill where another lorry that was passing in the other direction jump-started it with a rope, only for our lorry to break down again.

A large Mercedes car drew up and the driver, a local businessman, took us to the town of Goma. We arrived in the dark and did not know where to stay. We saw a small café, went in and ordered some food. Rob spotted two men about my age and walked over to have a chat. After a few minutes he came back with Gildas and Alain. We chatted with them in French and English and then Alain said, 'You must come and stay with our family.'

'Thank you, that is so kind of you,' I said in my best French. By now I had learned not to say the classic English 'Are you sure?' or 'I don't want to bother you'. This would be taken as an insult. They took us to their home where we met the rest of their family before having a very good sleep.

The next morning we sat and talked with Gildas, Alain and some of the family over coffee. They took us to their father's sewing shop in one of the main streets of Goma. Their father was working away on an old Singer sewing machine. There were two other Singer machines at the back of the shop.

'What are those machines doing here?' I asked.

Gildas translated for their father who said, 'These are broken and if I could get the parts I could repair them, employ more people and grow my business.'

'Where can you get the parts?' I asked.

'Maybe in Kinshasa,' he replied.

Gildas then said, 'Kinshasa is over one thousand six hundred miles away and it's not certain we could buy these when we got there.'

I thought about this and remembered that there was a Singer shop just off the Strand in London.

'When I get back to London I will go to the Singer shop and try and buy these for you,' I said. I got him to explain what the parts would do and what their names were in French. I took these details, wrote down the model numbers of the machines, even sketching little drawings of what the parts looked like and where on the machine they were needed. There were lots of smiles, thanks and backslapping all around, so no pressure.

Rob and I walked around the town. The street was littered with large rocks of lava from the 1977 eruption of nearby volcano Mount Nyiragongo when the lava flow covered eight square miles, destroyed 400 houses and reportedly killed 350 people. There were two parts to the town: one modern and affluent with large colonial-style houses leading down to Lake Kivu, and the other poorer with lots of shops and stalls and lava rocks in every street. Unsurprisingly, there was no lava on the roads of the affluent part of the town.

Goma has had a very challenging recent history. I had never heard of it before going there and I suspect few people in the UK had either. As a result of the Rwanda genocide at least 850,000 refugees arrived in Goma between June and August 1994. This was followed by a cholera epidemic. Wars have continued in eastern Congo pretty much ever since. As I was writing this I checked the UK Foreign Office advice, which stated, 'The security situation in eastern DRC remains unstable. There are continued reports of several towns... being attacked by or falling under temporary control of armed groups, including some territories and villages within a 30km range north of Goma. Armed groups are present and intercommunal violence can affect the political, security and humanitarian situation'[15]. This part of the world has suffered tragedy after tragedy for many years.

VOLCANO

On the way back to our hosts Rob and I discussed our plan to climb Mount Nyiragongo, the nearby volcano that had last erupted three years earlier. We had seen signs for guided tours and it looked like this was the only legal way to climb. Costs were priced for tourists far wealthier than us. We cooked up a plan, went to the market, bought some food, extra bottles of water and a warm blanket each.

By chance it was a Sunday when we set off. We did not know that this was the only day of the week that tours were not taken up the volcano, which was to our advantage. We left very early, thanking Gildas and Alain and their family. I left them postcards and reiterated my promise to visit the Singer shop in London. We started walking up the road to Kibati at the base of the volcano. Eventually we got a lift that dropped us off just before the village. Keeping an eye out for people watching we slipped into the forest

---

15   Foreign Travel Advice: Democratic Republic of Congo November 1, 2023. ⊘ gov. uk/foreign-travel-advice/democratic-republic-of-the-congo

and set off upwards. It was a steep climb from the start in very dense vegetation. There were paths but it wasn't clear which one to take. We carried on walking upwards, stopping occasionally for water and a bite to eat. We were completely in the shade with occasional shards of sunlight bursting through, and that meant insects. Mostly lots of gnats and ants that crawled into our sandals and itched like hell. It was hard work climbing. The path kept disappearing and we sometimes had to turn back and try another route up. We had to be careful not to trip over the thick vegetation. It was slow-going.

By mid-afternoon we arrived at the lava field, where very brittle, old black lava lay underfoot. There was no choice other than to walk across this very slowly to avoid getting our feet damaged by sinking into the lava as we trod. Every step had to be carefully planned. Looking back we were really foolish doing this without a guide. After about an hour of walking slowly up the lava field I suddenly realised that my tent was no longer tied to my rucksack. That was a blow. We might not survive the night without the tent.

I looked back and couldn't see it. The tent could be a long way back. We both swore and had a bit of an argument, which didn't last long as we both knew it was fruitless. Then I did something I'd never done before. 'I'm just going to shut my eyes and be silent for a minute,' I said to Rob.

I sat in silence and in a couple of minutes got an image in my mind of the tent by the trunk of a tree not far from where we were standing. I carefully walked down through the brittle lava and after 15 minutes I found it exactly in the place I had visualised.

'I've found the tent,' I shouted to Rob and climbed slowly back up.

'How did you know it was there?' asked a somewhat surprised Rob.

'I'm as surprised as you,' I said. 'I think that's what's called intuition.' Intuition is the ability to understand something instinctively, without the need for conscious reasoning. This was the first time I had even used the word or, more importantly, trusted that impulse. Ever since, being able to spot and act on intuition has been a key feature of my life. And it is something I learned climbing a volcano.

By now it was getting dark and we were near the summit of the mountain. We could tell by the thinness of the air. We were expecting to sleep in the tent, but fortunately found a small clearing with a wooden hut. We decided to spend the night there, eating our dinner of one banana and a bread roll shared between the two of us.

We woke up before first light and set off carefully for the summit, with a steep climb through a second tree layer and some very large ferns. When the trees thinned we had an incredible view. We could see the peaks of nearby mountains above the clouds. After an hour and a half we reached the summit, exhausted by the altitude and lack of food, but exhilarated as we looked down on the enormous crater. The crater was streaked with different colours, with a column of steam rising from a hole at its base. We lay on the rim and looked down. I had never seen anything like it. It was a magical moment.

After about 20 minutes we started to feel cold and set off to walk back down. On the way we spotted a group climbing up with guides, so quickly hid behind some large trees until they had gone. It was faster going back down and eventually we carefully came out of the trees, making sure that we weren't spotted. We sat down by the road and almost immediately a car arrived, slowing down to ask us where we wanted to go.

We had climbed 11,381 feet and looked down on an active volcano from the top of the crater. It was an unusual experience and an image I have retained. Nyiragongo has erupted many times since. A major eruption in 2002 produced paths of lava, one of which headed towards Goma. An estimated 300,000 people fled east to Rwanda, 245 died and some 120,000 lost their homes. There was another eruption as recently as 2021.

HILLS

Michel our driver wanted to discuss the politics of the area. 'President Mobutu[16] is a dictator,' he said, 'but the country is the safest that I can remember.' I was surprised how open he was about his views but careful not to share any opinions of my own. Michel carried on talking politics while driving along bumpy roads with thick green vegetation on either side opening up to views of mountains as he negotiated hairpin bends with deep drops below.

After a two-hour drive, we said goodbye to Michel at the town of Rutshuru. It was early afternoon, and we walked along an empty road, glad of the shade provided by trees and ferns. After an hour a lorry arrived and offered us a lift and we drove into the Virunga National Park, leaving this mountain range for a low, flat plain. We stood in the back of the largely empty lorry, holding on tight to the sides to avoid falling. We saw hippos lying by the riverbanks and lounging in the water. The lorry stopped at the small town of Rwindi where we thought we could stay overnight, but we didn't

---

16   Mobutu Sese Seko was President of the Democratic Republic of Congo from 1965 to 1971 and then President of Zaire from 1971 (when the country changed its name) until 1997 when he was deposed and exiled.

have a good feeling about it. After the tent incident on the volcano I was starting to trust these feelings. Soon we got a lift with a larger lorry as the road climbed up into the hills and mountains around more tight hairpin bends.

The view was stunning as we climbed up and up, looking down into the plain below that stretched into a distant haze. We kept climbing until we turned a corner into Kanyabayonga, a large mountain town. The hills were covered with thatched roofs as far as the eye could see. The centre of town was laced with narrow alleyways, similar to those of Lamu. We found a very basic room to rent for a tiny amount and cooked soup on Rob's stove.

The next morning we went for a walk in the town but again I had a bad feeling about it. For the first time on this journey I felt like an intruder. There was no obvious hostility and I couldn't really put my finger on it. There was a darkness about Kanyabayonga and I felt unsettled. I shared my feeling with Rob but this wasn't his experience. I decided to spend the rest of the day inside, something I hadn't done since I was ill with malaria. I gave this no further thought until many years later I read about massacres in Kanyabayonga in 1996, 2008, 2010, 2015 and 2022. This has been a town of great suffering.

I was ready to leave as soon as possible so we headed off early the next day to walk on the road north through the mountains. The atmosphere changed just a few miles up the road, as there were plenty of small villages with lots of people walking between them, always up for a chat. We conversed in simple French which even I could engage in. There was great food available to buy along the road, typically presented in little baskets outside homes. We ate strawberries, bananas, bread and peanuts. Every so often a lorry or large vehicle arrived, stopping to talk with us and typically giving us a lift a bit further along the way.

At one point we were joined by a teenage boy who was walking. 'Where are you from?' he asked. We explained our journey. 'You must come and stay at my village.' We walked with him for about an hour and then he went on ahead of us. About half an hour later we entered a tiny village with huts on either side of the road. Our companion was waiting with some of the villagers who invited us for dinner. We spoke to one of the men who seemed to be an elder and offered to pay for this; he said no, but asked if we could speak with the village about life in Europe. Of course we said yes and asked why.

'We are concerned about our young people leaving,' he said. After dinner we sat around a firepit which smoked a lot, keeping the mosquitos at bay. We spoke with most of the villagers in simple French about poverty, unemployment, racism and attitudes towards migrants. It was the beginning of something that became a feature of our journey through this country.

We found a rhythm. We woke early, packed up, ate a small amount, said goodbye and started walking. There were rarely vehicles in the morning, so we often walked for five or six hours. We walked through hills with small-scale agriculture and lime-green vegetation punctuating the cultivated areas. Banana trees were everywhere and the villages blended easily into the countryside. Intense rain fell for about thirty minutes each day. At first we would run for tree cover, but as the rain never lasted long, we started to adapt. I began to enjoy the daily soaking, getting wet while knowing that I would dry very quickly when the rain stopped and the humidity rose. We would hold up water bottles to fill them, which didn't take long and the water tasted so good.

Walking typically involved entertainment, with the laughter and screams of children, shouting 'tourist', 'pack man', and there was my favourite: 'howareyou'. The men and especially the women seemed to sing all the time with beautiful voices. And banana plants were everywhere, the leaves and fruit used for so many things – food, thatching for houses, baskets, boxes, raincoats, packaging and, in our case, toilet paper. I was cleaning my bottom with banana leaves and ferns which was easy as most of my toilet visits involved going into the forest and finding a quiet spot.

We walked 20 miles one day, arriving in the town of Beni as it got dark, feeling very stiff. We agreed that we would not walk so far the next day and would take a lot more breaks. A couple of lifts that morning helped with the miles and gave us some time to relax. One was in a very comfy car, which raced along the dirt road. Early afternoon we got a long ride in a lorry. It was very bumpy and the lorry was going a bit too fast for these roads. Over one bump we were thrown across the back of the vehicle and my left knee hit the side causing a large bruise.

At each stop the children provided entertainment. They would gather around but not too close and copy my facial expressions. So I made funny faces which they copied and then ran off roaring with laughter. It was as much fun for them as for us, and a lovely way of connecting with life in these villages. Despite the aches and pains, I had never had so much fun walking.

RAINFOREST

On the fourth day out of Kanyabayonga we descended from the hills into the Congo rainforest. There were so many different trees, ferns and vegetation, most of which I had never seen before. The

Congo rainforest covers an area of 500 million acres, making it the world's second-largest tropical forest. I had arrived at what was the heart of my journey.

We came to the small town of Komanda in the late afternoon. It had a significant crossroads in the middle. We arrived from the south. One road headed northeast to northern Uganda, one due east to southern Uganda and Kampala, and the third northwest and eventually to Kisangani and the River Congo. That was our road. We bought fruit and peanut butter, homemade in small, bite-sized balls, for our dinner and walked out on the road to find somewhere to sleep.

The next morning we walked about 10 miles on the dirt road through the rainforest. The road only stayed a road because the lorries drove through regularly enough to keep the trees from encroaching. Walking here was perfect. In the forest the roads were pretty flat, the tall trees kept the route mostly in shade and there was plenty of great company. The road was not just for vehicles, of which there were few; it was mostly used by local people walking from village to village, often carrying produce to sell at markets or visiting friends and family. There were conversations, singing and even music played as people walked.

That day we met some indigenous forest people (formerly known as pygmies) for the first time. They were smaller than us, with wrinkled faces, wearing loincloths and some carrying spears, bows and arrows. Most of the women had painted faces and bodies. They had small children with them. After they had had a good look at me and Rob they quickly folded back into the trees, disappearing into what looked like impassable forest.

We stopped at a village along the way and ate papaya while the local men vigorously debated something using their hands and bodies as much as their words. After a lot of walking, we were offered a ride on the top of a highly packed lorry, very similar to the way I had travelled in Sudan. Except that with the tree canopy encroaching, we had to lay very low most of the time. It was not long before the lorry broke down and we soon got a lift from another which would not start. All us passengers climbed down from the top of the lorry and pushed it for about 10 minutes before the engine started. By now there was a tailback of five lorries on the road that could not pass each other, turning into a convoy that drove slowly into Mambasa. Despite this it was a beautiful journey with birds and clouds of butterflies of every colour possible. When we got to Mambasa it was almost empty and felt like a ghost town. We were invited by a family to eat with them and sleep on their patch of land and, as previously, spent the evening around a fire talking about Europe.

The next day was a bit different. We travelled over 40 miles, half on foot and half on the back of a lorry. We arrived at the small village of Epulu mid-afternoon and went walking on a track into the forest, not knowing whether it was created by animals or people. We didn't have to walk far until we reached a clearing with smoke rising from nearby trees. We walked towards the smoke and came across an encampment of indigenous forest people.

I have never seen people living a life so close to nature before or since. There was a circle of 10 small huts the shape of small domes, made of branches and banana leaves. There were four men who immediately produced stools for us to sit on, made of four sticks with a circle of stalks holding them in place. There were women with black paintings on their legs. The children ran about. One of the men started to play a *likembe*, a type of thumb piano popular in Zaire. We could not understand their language but they gestured and took us into the forest where they hunted. I briefly wondered what would happen if they left us here but put that out of my mind. They had nets for catching monkeys, birds and wild pigs and they used their bows and arrows to kill these and more. They fished with spears in the small tributaries that would eventually end up in the River Congo. On this occasion a monkey was caught in a net and brought back to the circle of huts.

After a few extraordinary hours with these wonderful people it was time to leave. The sun would be down soon. One of the men escorted us on the path for a while and then pointed the way we should go back to Epulu. After he left we carried on walking back on the path until we met the road again. It was wet and at one point I accidentally walked into a muddy section. My whole foot sank into the mud. I didn't like this and instinctively felt that something was wrong.

Having returned to Epulu Rob and I ate a very simple dinner and talked about our experience of the day. We could not quite believe the generosity of the people we had spent time with. We both noticed that their settlement was clean and that there were no ants there unlike the forest around them. We were both transfixed by the children's dancing, the endless pounding of manioc (cassava) by the women, the body painting and their music. The collection of small huts fitted perfectly into the forest with its enormous, tall trees. Memories for a lifetime. And somewhere in the forest there is a postcard of a London monument.

We left Epulu the next day. That morning we decided that we would like to walk the whole day, even if we didn't get very far. We set off early and in no time were passing villages on the road and being joined by children who mimicked and mocked us, which we both enjoyed, and men who wanted to talk about Europe with us. There was a lot of fascination with life in Europe and a narrative that the 'streets were paved with gold'. That was not a fair description of life in Europe, particularly for migrants, and reminded me of our evening discussions.

We carried on walking and around the middle of the day came to a small village where we bought some of those delicious peanut butter balls for our lunch, a great walking food. We were also able to fill up with drinking water although were both a bit suspicious of it. We walked for the rest of the afternoon mostly with company. There was some sort of settlement every hour or so along the road. We politely turned down three rides, pushing aside thoughts that we might have nowhere to sleep the night. We need not have worried. As the sun started to fall in the sky, a young teenager approached us.

'My village is waiting for you, it is only twenty minutes' walk away,' he said. We set off with him and sure enough we soon arrived. The men and women of the village were waiting for us. The firepit was flaming and more importantly smoking to keep the mosquitos at bay. Food was being prepared and meanwhile Rob and I were each taken to a family home where we were shown where we would be sleeping the night and encouraged to hang our mosquito nets and lay out our bedding.

They even seemed to know we were vegetarian, as the meal was a stew of vegetables and beans on a bed of manioc. It was great, although I did struggle a bit with manioc, which I found quite slimy. We sat eating with the adults, about 20 of them. They asked us about where we were from and why we were walking through their forest. They were genuinely intrigued, although seemed surprised that two Westerners were travelling on foot.

As the meal drew to an end, one of the older men said, 'Will you please talk to our young people?' We both knew what he meant.

At this point the young people of the village came and sat around Rob and me and the adults left us. For the next hour we conversed with the teenagers. They spoke pretty good French, better than mine. Rob kindly translated when I was out of my depth. They shared their ambitions, which for many was to go to Brussels, Paris or London, where they thought they would find automatic wealth. We trod a fine line between telling them of poverty, unemployment, racism and attitudes towards migrants and on the other hand being supportive of their ambitions. The discussion turned to university education, which we were very supportive of, and in some cases using that education to make their country a better place. It was a good discussion and there was no mention of the fighting that had been a part of their early years. There was a sense that this was a good time for them to be coming into adulthood.

We had no idea then that the early 1980s would be a relatively peaceful time in this part of the world. That all changed with the civil wars that began in 1996 and have continued ever since in the Ituri region where we were travelling. In 2023 there were reports of eastern European mercenaries arriving in Goma, probably associated with the Wagner Group[17]. I can only hope that these young people we met survived this.

_____

17   dw.com/en/are-white-mercenaries-fighting-in-the-drc-conflict/a-64407711

After saying goodbye to the villagers, we set off on another day of walking and were joined by some of the young men we had spoken with the night before. We were a procession of six that of course attracted attention. For a while we continued the conversation of last night, discussing Europe, universities and opportunities. Then one of them brought out a *likembe* and started playing. This haunting sound echoed around the massive trees on either side and I felt like we were in a cathedral, a cathedral of nature. It was serene.

But there was a niggling pain in my right foot and although I could walk, I had a bit of a limp and with every step the pain was getting stronger. I tried to ignore this but eventually Rob asked me, 'What is wrong with your leg?'

'Remember the day we went to the indigenous settlement in the forest? I walked into a patch of mud on the way back,' I told him.

'Let's stop and have a look,' he said and I sat on the road while he inspected. 'There is something in the sole of your foot. We need to get this fixed.'

But how? We were deep into the Congo rainforest by now. Rob spoke with the guys who we were walking with and there was a long conversation. We were quite close to a village called Bakoma and they thought there was some kind of doctor there. We carried on walking and one of the guys went into the forest and returned with part of a tree branch that would be my walking stick. I hobbled on for a few more miles and we arrived in Bakoma.

The 'some kind of doctor' was Jake, an American medic volunteering for the American Peace Corps. He was not a doctor but had a substantial first aid kit. That made him a 'doctor' in these parts and was more than good enough for me. It was a stroke of luck that he was there. Jake was based in Kisangani and was visiting many of the villages in this region to do health checks. He had arrived in Bakoma two days previously.

'Let's have a look at your foot,' Jake said, after Rob had explained what he had seen. He examined my foot and said, 'Yes, there is some form of creature under your skin on your sole. I will try and remove it, but it will be painful.' I must have winced as he then said, 'Don't worry, I can offer you whisky as an anaesthetic.'

I drank a glass and bit on a clean rag he gave me while Rob held me tight to keep me as still as possible. Jake then proceeded to dig the creature out from the sole of my foot, place a plaster over the cut and bandage my foot up. It must have been painful but I don't really remember, probably because of the whisky. He showed me a huge creature, almost an inch long.

'I think we all need a drink now,' said Jake, pouring me another glass of whisky and one for Rob and himself. I could not believe my luck in finding him. And his bottle of whisky.

We stayed the rest of the day and overnight with Jake, this incredible, selfless man. He was intrigued about our trip and asked us a lot of questions about the villages and town we had walked through. He was fascinated that we had spent the afternoon with the indigenous people near Epulu.

'That's very unusual to spend time with them. I have been here a year and so far not met or seen any of them.'

'Maybe they don't like doctors,' I jokingly replied. 'I hear that they use the plants of the forest for medicine.'

'You must be feeling better,' said Jake.

We asked Jake a lot about the road to Kisangani and how we might travel up the River Congo.

'I hear that the ferry to Kinshasa is dangerous,' he said.

Rob replied, 'We met these British women, Claire and Sharon, who had taken the ferry from Kinshasa. They seemed OK.'

'I hear that it's notorious for robbery and pickpocketing. The Peace Corps won't let us travel on it,' replied Jake. We took his advice seriously.

In the morning my foot was feeling a lot better and I could walk, albeit more slowly and with more stops. Rob and I discussed what best to do and decided to start walking and hitch a ride if one came up. Thanking Jake, we set off and sure enough it wasn't long before we were joined by local people walking with us. It was always interesting and very motivating.

I began to realise that Rob's and my way of travelling was unusual and appeared to be appreciated by the majority of Zairean people that we met. It was clear that word had spread about these two scruffy young men walking through the rainforest and towards the end of each day we would typically be approached by people from the nearest village asking us to stay the night and talk with their young people. This was a real privilege for us. As always a postcard was left. For years I liked to think there were some of these on the walls on huts all over that part of the Congo rainforest, although sadly I suspect that given recent history that's very unlikely.

The next day we saw for ourselves how Western visitors typically travelled. About mid-morning a large open-sided lorry filled with seated travellers drove up the road. The passengers were leaning out, pointing their cameras with long lenses at the many people, including Rob and me, who were walking. The lorry shot past us, churning up the road and covering us and our co-walkers in dust. This started a conversation where it emerged that one of the reasons we were popular was that we did not take photographs. There was some fear of photos and many older people told us that cameras took their benevolent spirits away. This was interesting. Before I had set off I deliberated about bringing my camera, deciding not to as I thought it would get in the way of connecting with people. There had been many moments when I regretted not having a camera and many years later, while writing this book, my publisher was disappointed that I didn't have any photos of the journey. But it was the right decision and I'm glad that I had the foresight to offer my respect in that way.

One of the many interesting things about walking was seeing the differences between villages. Many were vibrant places where everyone seemed motivated. At some others people sat around, doing little and looking miserable. I talked to some of our co-walkers about this and got varying explanations. Some expressed negative views about the people of certain villages, something I have come across back home in Britain. Others talked about traumatic events related to the various wars in the region. And one just said 'malaria'. I instantly felt more compassionate towards these people. Trauma and illness were more than enough to generate the apathy and depression that I encountered.

The next day was a slow day as I could not walk fast or for too long, so it was good to hitch a long ride in the early afternoon which moved us forward on the road to Kisangani. We were dropped off mid-afternoon at Bafwatongono and we set off walking again. It felt easier for me after a couple of hours travelling in a vehicle. Sure enough late afternoon we were invited to stay in a village, eat and talk long into the night.

The following day took on the same pattern. We walked most of the morning, managed to hitch a ride around the middle of the day and then walked again late afternoon, before being invited to stay, share dinner and talk. We were getting into a rhythm but knew it would end soon. By the afternoon of the next day there was more traffic on the road and more people walking, often carrying goods and possessions on their heads, or pulling laden carts. There were many more villages and more food to purchase. We were approaching Kisangani.

We decided to try and hitch a ride into the town, which was a good move, and a very friendly businessman took us in his jeep. He told us a lot about Kisangani and its history, as well as great places to visit. Given the places he recommended, I suspected that he thought we were far wealthier than we really were. But he did drop us at the French Cultural Centre in the centre of town and close to the river. We went in and were offered a room at a very reasonable cost. We shared a twin bedroom with hooks for our mosquito nets, a fairly clean shared bathroom down the corridor, and to top it all, air conditioning. I had got used to sleeping drenched in sweat, so this was a treat.

That evening we went off to look around the town. We soon heard beautiful singing from what sounded like a choir. We followed the sound and quickly came to a church that was packed with people, all singing and clapping. There were drummers laying down a beat and a couple of guitarists. It was exciting, upbeat and very popular. We were invited in and enjoyed this dynamic and noisy form of worship.

Kisangani was the largest city we had been to since Kampala. The population in 1980 was 290,000. It is situated on the Congo River and is the end of the navigable part of that river for large waterborne cargo boats travelling the 1,060 miles from the capital

Kinshasa, making it a significant trading and strategic town. We walked around but I did not take to it in the way that I had Goma. We tried to speak with a number of local people but never really got very far. I didn't blame them – why should they be interested in two scruffy-looking Europeans?

ON THE RIVER

We walked down to the river to see the *pêcheries* where the Wagenya people fished using their ancestral and unique techniques. They had constructed a system of wooden tripods, anchoring them in holes created naturally in the rock by the river current, then fixing large conical traps with wooden scaffolding into the rapids. They then caught the fish from the traps by hand. It looked dangerous and every so often one of them fell in the water and swam back to the shore. They were great swimmers.

Later on we went to the port to see what our options were for getting a boat downriver to Bumba at the top of the bend in the Congo River. We had a crazy idea to travel down the river on a *piroc* (dugout canoe) but after we practised on one for an hour we agreed that we weren't strong enough. There was also the risk of contracting bilharzia if we capsized. Schistosomiasis (bilharzia) is a serious disease. Contact with fresh water containing a type of parasitic flatworm called schistosoma causes infection. Once absorbed these parasites live in the veins. Most of the eggs they lay are trapped in the tissues and the body's reaction to them can cause massive damage and often death.

The public ferry went from Kisangani to the capital Kinshasa each week. A pontoon ferry, much the same as the ferry on Lake Aswan between Egypt and Sudan, it was quite expensive. Jake, the

Peace Corps medic, had warned us off this. But we also saw quite a few private goods vessels and thought we might be able to hitch a ride on one of these. We had a few conversations with boat captains but no one was interested. We found the harbourmaster and asked his advice. 'The boats move in and out every day,' he said, 'so come again tomorrow morning. I'm confident that you will find a boat going to Bumba.'

That evening we went to an outdoor club where we were told the best band in Kisangani would be playing. They were fabulous, playing the best of Zairean music. The band was large, with musicians playing electric guitars, bass, saxophones, trumpets and congas, along with female and male singers with divine voices. The soulful music they were playing, *soukous*, had great dance rhythms but was often tinged with sadness. This is a part of the world that has suffered, and sadly continues to suffer, and the music felt at times reflective of this.

We went back to the port in the morning and started asking captains for a lift to Bumba. At the third attempt we walked up to a small diesel tugboat with four barges. There was a man who looked European on the jetty and we approached him.

'Are you travelling via Bumba?' asked Rob in his best French.

'I am,' he replied in perfect English. 'I assume you would like me to take you there?'

'Yes please,' we both replied.

'Yes, I can do that,' he said. 'I think it will take two days to get to Bumba. My name is Daniel and I'm from Israel. I have been taking goods up and down the Congo for three years.'

'Thank you so much,' we both said, introducing ourselves and explaining that this was part of a longer journey.

'I am not sure when we will depart but expect it to be later today. Please get your bags and come back as soon as you can,' said Daniel.

We went off to the Cultural Centre to get our bags and were back at the port before midday. Daniel showed us one of the barges. Cargo was typically stored below deck but this barge would be empty for the return trip so we could sleep there. We could cook on the barge as there was a small gas stove and there was a very rudimentary toilet. The boat had come up from Kinshasa with a full load on all four barges, but was going back with just two of these full. We went to a nearby market and bought enough food for the journey before returning.

The barges were tied up together beside each other, with the tug tied to a small jetty. That meant we could get on and off our barge by walking over the decks of the others and the tug, which was good, because the wait lasted the rest of the day and when night fell it was clear that we were not going anywhere. We slept on the barge and Daniel was nowhere to be seen. He had two crew and they indicated that he would be getting drunk in a nearby bar.

Darkness fell. We had eaten and got inside our mosquito nets before the mozzies arrived. We heard a noise outside and Daniel staggered on to our barge. He was drunk in so far as he was slurring his words and was a little unsteady on his legs. 'We leave at sunrise,' he announced. He produced a bottle of whisky and three small glasses and poured a drink for each of us, carrying on until the bottle was empty. So our first night on the River Congo involved getting drunk and listening to Daniel telling me what a terrible life he'd had since his wife had left him in Israel.

But he was true to his word and despite what must have been quite a hangover, we set off at sunrise. Rob and I helped the crew untie the barges and then tie them in a row, bow to stern, with the tugboat, named 'Moto', at the front. The crew of two had been joined by a river pilot, essential as there were shifting sandbanks all along the river.

Since leaving Israel I had travelled on foot, buses, trains, ferries, cars, lorries, *matatus*, *pirocs*, *dhow* and now a river barge. This small convoy of barges gently manoeuvred out of Kisangani and started down the majestic river. The Congo is the second-longest river in Africa. Along with its main tributary, the Lualaba, it is 2,715 miles long and its basin occupies 13% of the entire land mass of Africa. What first struck me was the width of the river. It was about one mile wide at Kisangani and apparently by the time it gets to Kinshasa it is over twice that. I had never seen anything like this.

We had a peaceful ride, although there were inevitable engine breakdowns, but nothing serious. On both banks of the river was dense rainforest with the occasional village. We passed quite a few families living in large dugout canoes. The children waved and shouted at us and we waved and shouted back. The tug steered a zigzag course down the river to avoid the sandbanks. It was a lovely day, ending with a breathtaking sunset over the water. As darkness fell this convoy of barges moored for the night. Anchors were dropped from each barge and then tied together with some slack in the ropes. Rob and I shouted 'goodnight' to the crew, captain and pilot across the water on the tugboat. We cooked up a simple supper and settled down for an uneventful night.

We set off at sunrise with the crew quickly getting the barges back into convoy formation. I spent most of the day sitting on the deck of our barge. It was mid-afternoon when the tugboat suddenly stopped and all the barges continued to move on, bumping into each other. Luckily no one fell into the crocodile- and bilharzia-infested water.

The tugboat had hit a sandbank. Although we had a pilot on board, the sandbanks in the Congo River move and shift all the time, a challenge even for an experienced river pilot. Captain Daniel decided not to listen to his pilot and instead got angry, taking his anger out on the sandbank by trying to reverse off it and then, even worse, trying to drive over it. The tugboat got more and more stuck on the sand and eventually, with much swearing, he gave up. By now it was close to sunset. Too late to do anything else other than stop for the night.

The sun fell out of the sky very quickly. In a few minutes a sunny day turned dark. I still could not believe how fast the sun set and rose, despite having been close to the Equator for over two months. It was very dark. And very quiet. The engine of the tugboat had stopped and there was no activity apart from muffled swearing in English. Except for the sound of the mosquitos. There had been a loud buzzing noise every night we had spent in the rainforest, and here over the stillness of the water it was even louder. We sat below deck inside our mosquito nets, knowing that the mosquitos would soon come. We ate a small meal of peanuts and dried banana. We did not know how long we would be stuck on the sandbank, so food had to be rationed. After eating Rob and I chatted a bit and then fell asleep.

I woke up in a sweat. It was dark and I was itching. That didn't feel right. I turned on my torch and was horrified. All I could see were mosquitos. They were all around the space we were sleeping in. I turned on my torch and in the beam there must have been many thousands of them, frantically flying around. But worst of all was that the mosquitos were inside my net as well as outside. There was a gaping hole in the net where I can only imagine that the sheer weight of the number of mosquitos had broken through.

There was nothing I could do. I got up and climbed on to the deck of the barge. I didn't dare turn on the torch again as that would attract more mosquitos, although I couldn't imagine more bites than I already had. To say that I was itchy would be an understatement. My body was on fire. I knew that scratching was the worst thing I could do but it was hard to resist. I could not dive into the river due to the risk of contracting bilharzia. There was nothing to be done but wait out the night.

When the sun rose I could see the extent of the damage. I had bites pretty much all over my body. Rob found an almost empty tube of bite cream in his tiny rucksack and I set about covering the worst of these bites. And then I took the small sewing kit from my rucksack and started to repair my mosquito net as best I could. All the time I had one thought on my mind. Malaria.

Meanwhile Daniel and the pilot had been busy. The crew were standing on the sandbank digging a channel to bring water up to the tug. One of the barges had an outboard motor, presumably carried for accidents like this. Sadly the river was not tidal this far east. There were multiple attempts by Daniel in the now motorised barge to pull the tugboat off the sandbank. For two hours there was no movement after each attempt so then the crew would dig more sand and then he would try again. Eventually the tug started to move a little and an hour later it was back afloat. Rob and I were anchored a little way off with the remaining three barges, with a grandstand view. We cheered along with everyone else.

We set off again having lost some time and as the sun started to set we arrived at Bumba. As it was late Daniel said he would load up in the morning and suggested we stay the night on the barge. We were delighted as it saved looking for somewhere and we set up for the night. I hoped that my repairs to the mosquito net would work. They did, but I was itching so much that it was difficult to sleep.

BACK IN THE FOREST

We left the barge in the morning, thanking Daniel and the crew. Almost immediately we got a lift on a lorry which dropped us off after an hour. We started walking. After a few miles we arrived in a village where a church service was in full flow. The church was a large shed with no walls, open to the outside. It was packed with people who were all singing and swaying to a beat provided by six musicians playing guitars, drums and rattles. Bunting all over the church was swinging with the music and it looked like the church itself was swaying.

Rob and I approached and some of the people waved at us to join in. The service was mostly music; even the occasional short periods of prayer were spoken melodically. I've been to church and other religious services in my life but I have never felt so uplifted by religion as on that day. It was magical, spiritual, natural and a celebration of life in one of the poorest places on earth. After the service quite a few of the congregation gathered around and spoke with us. They wanted to know all about our travels, where we had been and why we were doing this. They offered us something to eat and then we set off walking again, with some of the younger members of the congregation joining us for the first mile or so.

After about an hour's walking a lorry stopped and picked us up. It was a beautiful drive through the rainforest. One of my most vivid memories of the whole trip is of that afternoon. As the lorry was driving, clouds of butterflies of all colours flew up from where the tyres met the dirt of the road, enveloping the sides of the vehicle. It was the most colourful show I had ever seen.

The lorry drove us into Lisala and we found a simple hostel to stay the night and a food stall where we ate our first hot meal in two days. Beans and manioc, of course. My itching had calmed down a bit. The most exciting thing about Lisala was that I managed to buy a far superior mosquito net. Rob was so impressed with it that he bought one too.

The next day was one of the hardest days yet. We set off at five in the morning thinking we might get a lift with an early-morning lorry. We walked almost 10 miles and came to a village where we were told that the mosquitos only disappeared for four hours a day. The mood of the people was very low there and I could see that a lot of people had malaria.

We hitched a ride on the first lorry we saw, which was headed to Gemena, about 60 miles further on. This lorry was very full of people and everyone was standing crammed together in the back. We stopped in the afternoon to cross a river on a small ferry which was fine, but then the trouble started. First a heavy sack of grain fell on my foot that was still recovering from the parasite. Then as we were getting back on to the lorry after the ferry crossing a man jumped on, landing on my head. As he did, all his luggage emptied over me including two litre-bottles of petrol. My clothes were soaked and I was miserable. I tried to be calm but one of the other passengers started remonstrating with him and there was a fight. Luckily at that moment the lorry lurched and everyone had to hang on tight which defused the moment.

Thankfully it wasn't too long before we got to Gemena where one of the other passengers suggested that we walk up to the Catholic Mission which might put us up for the night. We were welcomed by nuns who were so friendly, taking pity on us and particularly me in my clothes stinking of petrol. They led us each to a room of our own with clean white sheets, showed me to a bath and, while I soaked away weeks of dirt, washed my petrol-soaked clothes. They gave me clothes to wear and took us to dinner in their dining room. And in all of this generosity there was no demand to pay or even pray. They were so kind. I was brought up a Christian but left the faith in my late teens. That night I was really touched by their kindness. I had my best sleep since Lamu.

The next few days were much more relaxed and we returned to the rhythm that we had entered into before Kisangani. We walked in the morning, typically with co-walkers who were moving from village to village or en route to foraging or hunting in the forest. We joined some of them one day and discovered herbs that were used to bring down fever. Around the middle of the day we typically managed to hitch a lift and walking later we would be approached to stay the night in a village, complete with food and talking with the young people.

SHOTS ACROSS THE WATER

It was our last day in Zaire and we were heading towards the border. We needed to get there soon, as our visas expired that day. As we got closer the forest started thinning out and we could see small grassy hillocks, fields and signs of agriculture. We eventually arrived at Zongo on the Ubangi River, the border between Zaire and Central African Republic (CAR). It was a tiny place, with a few shacks and a run-down immigration building with the roof falling in. It was quite chaotic. On the shore were a number of dugout canoes which were the only means of transportation across the river to the modern city of Bangui that we could see in the distance.

We were very relaxed going into immigration, our passports were fine and we got our exit stamps. The problem came when we reached the customs office, which was a tent on the shoreline. The customs official looked at our passports and then asked for our currency declaration forms. No problem, as we had got these signed at the bank in Goma where we had changed dollars into zaires, the currency. We handed the forms over.

'You have not spent enough,' he said. Rob, who spoke the best French, explained how we had travelled and that we had not spent very much money. This didn't work and the customs official became angry. He demanded that we pay a lot more, basically all the money we had. This sounded like a demand for a bribe. Luckily he had not taken our passports, which were back in our passport bags around our necks and under our shirts.

The customs tent was right by the dugout canoes and we had the exit stamps that we would need to enter CAR. The official went outside and walked to the immigration building. This could get very complicated. Rob said, 'Let's get in this dugout.'

There was one moored a few feet away and we ran in and told the ferryman to set off immediately. He got going at some speed. We were halfway across the river, which was fairly wide at that point, when we saw lots of activity on the Zairean side. Men were shouting and waving at us. Then a shot was fired.

We looked back and saw more shots hitting the water and only just missing our dugout canoe.

'*Plus vite, plus vite!*' Rob shouted at the ferryman.

DEMOCRATIC REPUBLIC OF THE CONGO

In the 1990s the Rwandan civil war and genocide had a significant impact on Zaire and in 1997 Rwandan and Ugandan forces invaded. President Mobutu fled and opposition leader Laurent Kabila marched into Kinshasa, declaring himself president and reverting the name of the country to the Democratic Republic of the Congo (DRC). Since the late 1990s, conflict in eastern DRC has led to approximately six million deaths [18]. As of 2024, the country is the fourth-poorest in the world [19].

18 cfr.org/global-conflict-tracker/conflict/violence-democratic-republic-congo

19 gfmag.com/data/economic-data/poorest-country-in-the-world

6

CENTRAL AFRICAN REPUBLIC, CAMEROON AND NIGERIA

CENTRAL AFRICAN REPUBLIC

GUNSHOTS AND PARATROOPERS

We were in Central African Republic (CAR) territorial waters by the time the shot was fired. We looked back and saw more shots hitting the water and only just missing our dugout. The boatman paddled even faster and the shots on the water receded. In no time we were on the riverbank at Bangui. To our surprise a French paratrooper in khaki combat uniform, a red beret and with a sub-machine gun walked down to meet us.

'What was that all about?' he asked. Rob explained what had happened with the customs official and the paratrooper replied, 'Don't worry, it happens all the time. This is an extortion racket which they try on foreign travellers.' He went on to tell us that shooting was less common but that they would have known that the shot would not have reached us and that it was done for show.

'Will the boatman get into trouble?' I asked.

'Not at all,' the paratrooper replied. 'They regularly take people across the river who the customs officers try to extort. It's all part of the show.'

My heart rate had shot up and despite the explanation took a while to calm down. I'd had a gun pointed at me on a few occasions, but I had never been shot at before. It was one of many firsts on this journey and one I would prefer not to repeat.

He smiled and then welcomed us to CAR and walked with us to the immigration office, which was a lot smarter than the Zongo centre. We were each issued with a temporary entry visa and told to attend the Ministry of the Interior within five days to get a full visa to visit the country.

Then we entered Bangui. The centre, by the river, was modern, with wide tarmac roads, long avenues of trees, roundabouts and low buildings. We could see the French legacy immediately. The shops were full of goods, there was wealth on display and there were many

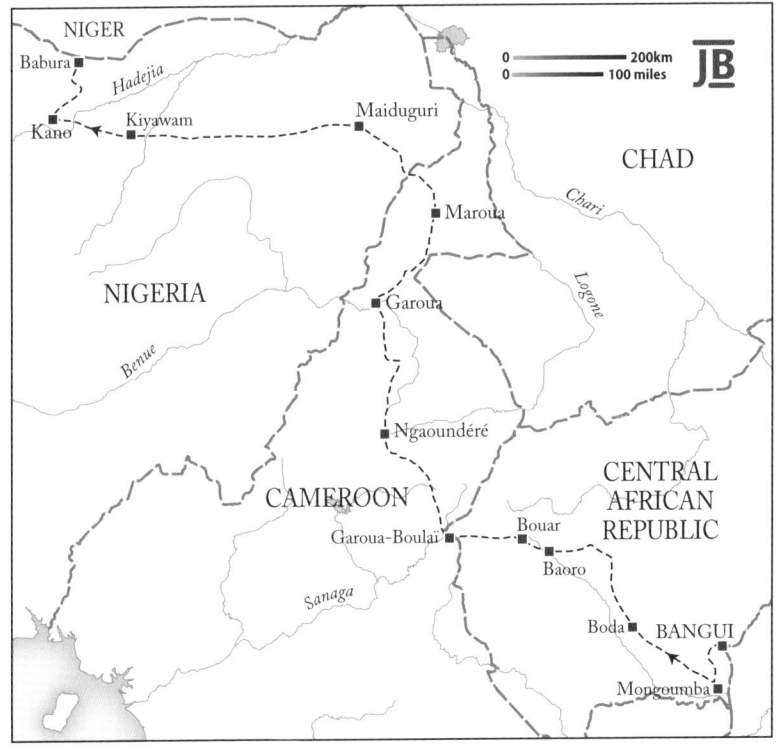

more Europeans around, more than I had seen anywhere on the journey. And it was expensive.

We found a very basic room to stay, a shed with a dirt floor in a poor area of the city. There was a rough communal toilet in the yard with no door. It was somewhere to sleep but we would have to find somewhere else soon.

There was a post office with a Poste Restante, so I was able to get mail for the first time in a long time. I had 12 letters from my parents and sisters as well as friends from Bristol whom I had written to ages ago.

So why were there French paratroopers in Bangui? Jean-Bédel Bokassa was a military leader who became president of the country after leading a coup in 1966. He declared himself Emperor in 1976 and was known for his cruelty and extravagance. In September 1979 there was a bloodless military operation led by France to depose Bokassa and reinstate the exiled former president. By the time we arrived in Bangui 10 months later the French paratroopers were maintaining law and order, but the politics were still unstable. Despite this, the city appeared to carry on a normal life, albeit with paratroopers with guns ever present.

Rob met a French teacher who invited us to stay at his large house in the city. It was really lovely with use of the kitchen, swimming pool and a great music system. This was the most luxurious place I had stayed all year. Rob and I went a bit over the top on little luxuries such as French chocolates and even eating in a restaurant one evening. I bought a couple of shirts in the market as my last decent one never recovered from the petrol soaking. I spent some time by the pool writing replies to all my friends and family, but not telling my family about the shooting.

Rob and I needed visas for CAR as we only had the temporary ones, so after five days we headed off to the interior ministry where they gave us only fourteen days from the day we arrived. That wasn't a lot of time, leaving us only nine more days in the country. We also obtained visas for Cameroon, our next destination.

This brought to a head a discussion that had been bubbling under for a while. Rob and I had been travelling together since Lamu. We didn't always agree on what we wanted to do. I had begun to find him a bit irritating and he was feeling the same way. We sat and had a coffee in one of the French-style cafés and agreed to go our separate ways for a while. We both felt sad and agreed that we wanted to meet up again after a break. We decided to meet in the Cameroonian city of Ngaoundéré on August 15th, two days after we would have to have left CAR and a reasonable 170 miles from the border. We also agreed that whoever got there first would wait at least two days for the other, after which we could carry on with our respective journeys. We felt closer than we had for some time, while at the same time I felt relieved at the thought of travelling alone for a bit. Little did I realise what lay ahead.

ON MY OWN

Rob left two days later. He headed northwest to the border with Cameroon. I had done some planning, given the time restraint of the visa, and estimated that I would have time to travel to Mongoumba, a small town on the Ubangi River about 75 miles south of Bangui. This was in the opposite direction to Cameroon, but I had heard that there were indigenous tribes in the area. Spending the short time in the indigenous village in Zaire had been a real highlight for me and I just wanted one more opportunity to meet with indigenous people before I finally left the rainforest.

I walked out of the city and very quickly got a lift from a UNDP (United Nations Development Programme) lorry. My mood, which had been low in the city, lifted as soon as I was back in the forest again. The UNDP team stopped a few times en route at the neat plantation and forestry villages. I enjoyed travelling with them as they told me a lot about the development and economic challenges in CAR following the devastation created by Bokassa.

We came to the river near Mongoumba and I said goodbye to the UNDP. They were intrigued that I wanted to visit indigenous people. I walked to the river where there were plenty of *pirocs* and paid for a ride across. Once on the other side I was back in the rainforest with its sounds and smells that felt so familiar. By a stroke of luck I met three young local men, one of whom said, 'Come with us; we will take you to the village. We are going to a ceremony to commemorate the death of an indigenous elder.'

I was touched that the local people held their elders in such respect. 'Will it be appropriate for me to attend?' I asked.

'Yes, the more people who give their respects the better it will be for the afterlife of the elder,' he replied.

When we arrived at the village it was much larger and more permanent than the one I had been to near Epulu. Many of the men wore a piece of Western clothing (shorts and T-shirts) but the women and children wore the traditional small loincloth, typically made of a bunch of leaves. They did not have painted bodies but many had patterned scars on their faces and stomachs. Most of the men and women had shaved heads with little tufts of hair sticking above their foreheads.

Women, men and children were dancing in a line around the settlement, swaying to the beat of the drums and rattles, singing and wailing as they went. As the men moved they did a type of shivering that moved all the way up and down from their feet to their heads. The women and girls swayed and shuffled in perfect unison, singing in perfect pitch. There were two albino women who were the most boisterous of them all, eagerly showing off their moves. This was very different from most of the albino people I had encountered so far on my journey, who had often looked so shamefaced as they were typically marginalised. Later the chief gave a speech translated for me by one of the men who brought me to the village. He said that the dance would raise good spirits who would protect the tribe and respect the dead.

When the celebration was over my three friends for the day took me to see some other of the smaller indigenous villages. There were women pounding the manioc and squeezing oil out of the palms. The men smiled and encouraged us to sit with them and drink a form of beer. Not a great taste but an honour to be offered this.

After a really memorable afternoon, my three friends and I walked back to the river. We all went back across and walked into the town of Mongoumba. Onc of them took me back to his family home and they kindly put me up for the night in a small shed at the back of their house. It was only when I got there that I realised I had temporarily travelled into Zaire illegally, as the river is the border.

I spent the next four days travelling on minor dirt-track roads. As far as the town of Boda I was still in the rainforest but after that the trees thinned out and there was more agriculture and larger villages. I got back into the rhythm of walking most of the day, getting a lift for part of the journey and staying the night in a village, talking into the night. I found that I could do this on my own, without needing someone else to travel with or translate. One of the great joys of travelling alone was that I met people whom I enjoyed travelling with. In particular I had enjoyed travelling with Rob and Henk on this journey but I needed this time on my own. I enjoyed being able to make my own decisions. I walked a bit less every day, especially in the middle of the day as it was very hot and humid. I had more contact with people and my French improved significantly.

I had set off on this journey a young, naïve white man who lacked confidence. But in travelling I found I needed to start up conversations with people I had never met before. I needed to stand up for myself in tricky situations. And I had to ask for help when I was in trouble. All this was new for me. And the more I did these things the richer my journey became. I started to build a quiet confidence in myself that set me up for the rest of my life.

I headed from Boda towards a village called Carnot but soon heard that the road was closed so turned around and walked back the way I had come. Finally a lorry gave me a lift to Yaluke, getting me much closer to Bouar and towards the border with Cameroon. We passed and sometimes stopped at villages along the way. They all had little markets where I could buy peanuts, peanut butter and dried bananas which I became a fan of and still am. On the road there were butterflies of every colour possible, with clouds of them appearing as a lorry or car passed and even when I was walking. I've never seen so much colour. Many had wings like surrealist paintings, others that were like line drawings of clouds. This was some of the best walking of my whole journey and I was rarely alone as local people walked the roads so much. I always felt safe walking forest roads.

After another beautiful day's travelling, I spent what I thought would be my last night in CAR with a family in a village just outside the small town of Baoro, close to Bouar, where I needed to get a ride on to the Cameroon border at Garoua-Boulaï. It was a journey of 125 miles and the road was in pretty good condition with plenty of traffic, so I was confident that I would get to the border before my visa expired at the end of the following day.

KINDNESS OF STRANGERS

I woke up early with a mild headache and a strained feeling in my eyes. I put it down to tiredness, although a little part of me was suspicious that this was something worse. But I was determined to continue travelling and said my goodbyes to the family I stayed with, leaving them one of the London postcards as a gift.

I set off walking along the road but quickly felt much worse and after about 30 minutes I collapsed at the side of the road. I was still conscious but all the energy seemed to have left my body. I have no idea how long I lay there but eventually heard some noises. A vehicle had stopped and there were people talking. A hand came down and helped me into a car. I had the presence of mind to check that my bag was with me and then they drove off with me collapsed on the back seat.

There was an intense discussion between the two men in the front of the car. I could not make it out as they spoke in a combination of French and Sango, the two official languages of the country. I was very dizzy and not doing well at all, but as far as I could gather they were worried about being seen with me in case there were official repercussions. I tried to talk in French to them, but no sound seemed to come out of my mouth.

We arrived in a larger town that I assumed must be Bouar and they helped me out of the car into a street that had nice detached houses with small gardens. They told me to get help and drove off. I forced myself to stagger up to houses and ask for help but most people looked frightened. I don't blame them – it could have been dangerous if a European died on their watch. And I must have looked ghastly.

Eventually I walked up to a house that was bigger than the others. As I approached a man came out, took one look at me and said, 'Please come in and rest at my house.'

'Thank you,' I said as he took my arm and walked me down to a small building in the garden. I sat while he set up a bed with a mosquito net and I dragged myself in. By now I had a terrible headache, my eyes ached and I was sweating with a fever. My throat was really dry and to cap it all I had diarrhoea.

I must have spent the rest of the day in and out of sleep. It was a relief to be on a bed but I was in a strange, depressed altered state. I started hallucinating and what I saw was scary. Sometime in the night I had a brief moment of lucidity. I had malaria but much worse than last time. And then I remembered the night on the Congo River when the mosquitos broke through my net. It was about three weeks ago. The incubation period in most malaria cases varies from seven to thirty days.

In the morning, I felt much worse. Michael who had taken me in the day before was a Regional Director of L'UNICEF en République Centrafricaine, the national branch of UNICEF. He could see I was pretty ill so got me up and drove me to the pharmacy in town. He was a well-known figure and must have used his influence to get me treated quickly. I was given an injection of Quinimax and would have to come back for another one the next day.

I wasn't really aware of all this but Michael told me afterwards. I am so lucky to have met him and in rare moments of lucidity I felt so grateful to him and his family. I can't imagine how I would have managed to get treatment without him. I forgot that I was now in the country illegally.

But most of the time I was feeling terrible. Despite eating nothing I was sick on a regular basis until eventually there was nothing left to come up. The headache was the worst I have ever experienced, my stomach hurt, my throat was raw and to add insult to injury the injection in my buttock made that very painful. Malaria is a really nasty disease and yet I was one of the lucky ones – I was getting treatment.

Later that afternoon my headache had subsided quite a bit, but my stomach was still painful, especially when I coughed, which was a lot of the time. The injection must have been working despite, or perhaps because of, the pain in my buttock. That night I had a feverish night of hallucinations and nightmares. There were monsters in the room, I was eaten alive by millions of mosquitos, I had parasites under my skin. And more that, thankfully, I can't remember.

The next morning Michael woke me up and took me to the pharmacy for my second injection. He saw me getting dressed and when we got back announced that I must eat something. His command suggested that I must have looked very thin so I ate a bowl of vegetable and bean soup, managing to keep it down. Despite the pain now in both buttocks, I did start to feel a little better, although the rest of the day was rough as the fever and headache returned for a while. I felt so helpless and cried for the first time in a long time. I definitely wouldn't meet up with Rob in Ngaoundéré; by the time I got there he would be long gone.

I woke after a better night's sleep and was much calmer, with no headache. After Michael took me for a third injection he asked me if I would like a bath. That sounded amazing. He lit a fire in a pit outside his house and once it was burning he and his eldest son lifted a huge metal tub on to a metal frame suspended over the fire. They were heating the water. Once the water was warm enough, he asked me to undress and climb in, which I did. Once I was in the whole family came out of the house to have a look at the white man in the bath. It was very moving and I was so grateful to them all as I wiped away my tears.

Then Michael's wife brought out a large towel and the whole family turned around while I got out and wrapped myself in the towel. She went into the house and came out with my clothes, all washed and folded. After I had dressed the family brought out food and we ate together outside. The children wanted to practise their English on me which I thought was very good, much better than my French. Towards the end of the afternoon Michael and I sat and he spoke about his work for UNICEF. I remain a regular donor to UNICEF to this day.

I left Michael and the family two days later. I gave each of the children a postcard of London, so they had a few of the landmark sites. I wished I was able to give the family something and asked if there was anything I could send from the UK, thinking of the man with the sewing shop in Goma.

Michael thought for a minute and said, 'There is nothing we need, we have a good life.' And then, 'We were so glad to be able to help you get well again.' I asked for their address and it's still in the back of my diary. I have written many times but never heard anything from him. I try not to worry about this.

I will never forget Michael, but my overwhelming experience throughout this entire journey was that I received great kindness and generosity from complete strangers. For much of the trip, as a backpacking white man travelling on foot, lorries and public transport, I was a rarity, and people were interested in what I was doing. And there is no doubt – I simply could not have made this journey without the lorry and car drivers, villagers, café and hostel owners, policemen and officials, doctors and many others who offered me a place to stay, medication, company and more. Some 45 years later I feel such gratitude for every one of those people.

BORDER LUCK

I thanked Michael and his family profusely and walked off to the bus stop. I thought that walking and hitching would be a bad idea as I was still quite weak, although really grateful to be well enough to travel again. The bus was full of people from CAR, Cameroon, Nigeria, Niger and Senegal. It was a beautiful journey over hills and through valleys filled with mist. The bus had 'Super Boeing 747' painted on its sides – although it was neither spacious nor fast. I sat next to various people including an Arab woman with the smallest baby I had ever seen, much smaller than either of my sisters when I first saw them.

After about three hours the bus arrived at the customs post. I was a bit anxious as I had outstayed my visa by five days and was not sure of the potential consequences. I imagined a bribe at the least and hopefully not gunshot like at the last border. All passengers had to get out of the bus with our baggage, show passports and have our baggage checked. I tried to appear relaxed as the official examined my passport, flicked through the pages and then waved me through. He either did not spot the date or he could not read. I quietly breathed a sigh of relief and stepped back on to the bus.

But half a mile down the road the bus stopped again. It was a second CAR customs post. The same procedure took place all over again. We all exited the bus and queued up to have our passports or identity papers checked by one customs official. And yet again I was waved through. Unbelievable.

Once again the bus set off and once again we stopped. This time it looked like the actual border. There was a barrier across the road. In the distance I could see another barrier and the Cameroon national flag. So this was the final border and I suspected that the more efficient customs officials would be here.

Everyone got off the bus. So we were leaving the country now. I joined the queue and was really anxious. There were three officials and a couple of French paratroopers in the background, machine guns over their shoulders.

The officials were having short conversations with most of the passengers ahead of me in the queue before stamping their passports or papers and waving them through. When my turn came the official looked at my passport, flicking through the pages that were by now full of stamps. He looked intently at each page and then raised his head to face me.

'I hope you enjoyed visiting our country,' he said.

'Yes sir, it's a wonderful country,' I replied.

'Very good, I hope you come back again soon,' he answered.

'I look forward to coming back again,' I said. And with that he smiled, stamped my passport and I was through.

Incredible!

FAILING STATE

Central African Republic today is close to a failed state. Armed groups control large parts of the county. What was the Wagner Group now provides security for the president in exchange for the exploitation and export of mineral and other resources. The United Nations Office for the Coordination of Humanitarian Affairs estimates that approximately half of CAR's population are experiencing acute food insecurity. This is despite significant natural resources of gold, oil, uranium and diamonds. It is a terrible example of a potentially wealthy country inhabited by very poor people and at the time of writing is the third-poorest country in the world[20]. UNICEF still has a presence there.

CAMEROON

CATCH-UP

I was elated that I had made it through the three customs checks without any problems, despite having overstayed my visa by five days. I left the CAR customs building and walked as swiftly as I could to the Cameroon side, but without rushing in order not to cause any second thoughts. The gate was raised and a French paratrooper waved me through.

The gate was already raised at the Cameroon side of the border and I walked through to the customs shed there. This was easy as I had acquired a 15-day visa in Bangui that I thought would be more than sufficient. This was my first day on the road since the malaria

---

20 gfmag.com/data/economic-data/poorest-country-in-the-world

and I was very tired, so found a hostel to stay in, had a shower and went out to eat all before the sun started to set. I slept well.

The next morning I was keen to get to the town of Ngaoundéré on the off chance that Rob was still there, so I got ready as soon as I woke up. I bought some food and walked out of the town hoping for a ride. A Land Rover stopped almost immediately, driven by Jacques, a French engineer who was heading to Ngaoundéré. He was happy to take me there, which was a great relief as I was not sure how long I could walk or whether I was up for the rigours of travelling on the top of a lorry.

'What are you doing here?' he asked. 'It's very unusual to see Western travellers coming out of CAR.'

'How long have you got?' I asked.

'Well, it will take about five hours to get to Ngaoundéré, so why don't you tell me everything?' replied Jacques.

So I did. It took most of the five hours including the many questions that Jacques asked. Some that I remember included:

'How did you manage to hold on to the ropes on top of the lorry for so long?'

'How on earth did you manage to eat the sheep's eye without getting sick?'

'Were you anxious travelling in Uganda? It sounds very dangerous.'

'Do you think you've been very lucky, despite being shot at, contracting malaria and more?'

On either side of the road was scrubland and trees and bushes that were smaller than I had been used to. There were areas of forest in the distance and some evidence of farming. The dust road was reasonably good and when we reached Ngaoundéré Jacques dropped me in the middle of town saying, 'That is one of the most interesting drives I have ever had.'

'Thank you so much,' I replied as I climbed out of his Land Rover. I walked to the nearest café and almost immediately a couple of men came up to me and said, 'Rob left yesterday. You must be Patrick.'

We sat down and had a coffee. They were brothers named Florent and Christian and they told me that Rob had stayed with them. He had waited a few days for me before heading off. They said he had been a bit worried about what might have happened to me. I told them that I had got stuck in CAR with malaria and told them all about how Michael and his family in Bouar had looked after me. They asked loads of questions and then invited me to stay the night with their family. When I got back to their house there was a note from Rob waiting.

> *Hello Patrick. I'm sorry to miss you, I was looking forward to travelling with you again. I hope that it's not illness that has delayed you. I am heading north via Garoua to the Nigerian border, on to Kano and then north into Niger. I have no idea when I will get there but will leave messages along the route and hopefully we will meet up. Rob*

I was really touched by this message. I had rather felt that Rob, as the more experienced traveller, would prefer to travel on his own, or perhaps with someone else. On reflection this was probably my insecurity rather than the truth. It also presented me with a decision. I had planned to travel to the capital Yaoundé to get visas to travel through Nigeria, Niger and Algeria. I had assumed that Rob would have gone further on ahead after my delay and didn't expect that he would want to meet up again after I had missed him here. Over dinner with Florent and Christian and their family I discussed all of this.

'I'm not sure I can catch up with Rob,' I said.

'You must go and find Mr Rob,' said Christian. Florent agreed and the whole family nodded. It was really sweet that they were so invested in our travelling together again. They had been looking for me ever since Rob had told them about me. They had told all their friends to look out for me and some of them came around to the house later. I gave them a potted history of my journey thus far in my best French. There were sighs at the story of kindness in CAR and shrieks when I spoke of the shooting at the border. Mostly they wanted to hear all about countries that they had never been to. Of course I was going to find Rob now. I felt almost like I was travelling with him already.

But despite the enthusiasm of that evening, I still had the visa problem to deal with. Christian and Florent had a long chat with their father, who didn't speak much French, and then Florent said, 'Father thinks you could get a Nigerian visa in Garoua.'

I went to sleep that night with a lot to think about. I slept for a while, woke up early and decided to take a risk and head to Garoua and see if I could get visas for Nigeria, Niger and maybe Algeria. Looking back I am amazed how relaxed I was about this. These days I like my travelling to be well organised and not as hardcore. Maybe that's a fact of age – I'm 67 years old, no longer 22. But something was happening to me. I was becoming more relaxed about taking risks. I had taken a few on this trip and survived so far. Without realising it at the time, I was setting myself up for what was going to come when I returned home.

NIGERIA

The next three days were a whirlwind. I travelled 770 miles in three days and made one border crossing. That was an average of 256 miles a day compared with 186 a day travelling from Khartoum to Juba in Sudan. It was all a bit of blur. I did get a Nigerian visa in Garoua, which fortunately had a consulate due to its proximity to the border. I stopped overnight at Maroua in northern Cameroon and crossed the border to Nigeria the next morning, passing through the town of Maiduguri and staying the night at Kiyawam after a punishing twelve-hour drive on the back of a lorry. I wore a headscarf the whole way to keep the sun and dust off me as best I could.

These are names of towns that probably sound distant. But they are places known for abduction and massacres by terrorist groups. In 2014 the Chibok kidnapping of 276 mostly Christian female teenage students by Boko Haram was in this area. And that's not all. In 2015 suspected militants attacked nearby Ngamdu, a town that I passed through. It is still one of the most dangerous places in the world. The UK Foreign Office has an 'advice against all travel' warning for all of northeast Nigeria and the border regions of Cameroon. Not a journey that could easily be made today.

But this was 1980 and my experience of the area was of a beautiful and peaceful place. It was a predominantly Muslim region with villages made up of bell-shaped mud huts surrounded by straw walls. It was a different type of travelling because it was so fast and I was barely walking at all. Just as well, as it was around 35 degrees in the middle of the day and unlike in the rainforest there was little shade. But it was only four days since I had left Michael and his family and I was weaker than usual. In retrospect it was foolish of me to be doing so much travelling so soon after such an intense illness.

Around midday I arrived in Kano, the second-largest city in Nigeria. I was not sure whether I needed a visa to enter Niger so asked around if there was backpacker hostel. I found one and luckily there were a few travellers who had come from Niger. I sat with them and talked about visas and travelling conditions. The consensus was that the Niger government would issue a visa at the border. Algeria was another matter. No one had a clear position on this. I decided to see how things went, one step at a time. I had hoped that I would hear news of Rob but I didn't meet anyone who had heard of him. I decided to head in the direction that his note had suggested.

I stayed a night at the hostel because I had one important task to do before travelling north into Niger. I was worried about the El Arish stamp in my second passport which had nearly meant that I didn't make it to Sudan or beyond. My first passport was almost full of visas and other stamps and I would probably need the second one. I found a market stall that sold sewing materials and bought a tiny set of scissors and spent the evening carefully cutting the page with the difficult entry stamp out without destroying the binding. I counted on no one spotting the gap in the page numbers.

In the morning I set off for Niger. Nigeria was an easy country for hitchhiking and I had a number of lifts to get to the border. My final lift was with Farid, an Algerian miner heading to Arlit, the uranium mine in the north of Niger. With every mile the trees became sparser and the land less green. We reached the border in the late afternoon.

7

NIGER

ARRESTED

I crossed the border soon after I got there. It was not much of a place and there were plenty of soldiers with guns. Unusually for this trip I was given my visa on the spot, without having to go to an embassy. There were a few shared taxis on the Niger side, so I climbed into an almost full taxi, a desert version of a *matatu*. It was late, and I didn't like the idea of staying at the border.

The taxi stopped in a village called Tinkim, a nice place consisting of low mud houses. There was lots of great food for me to eat including eggs and, to my great excitement, a locally made cheese. I hadn't eaten cheese for a long time. There was nowhere to sleep so I took a chance from my Sudanese experience and went to the police station and asked if I could stay the night there. The two policemen on duty said yes immediately and I slept in a simple straw hut at the rear of their office.

The next morning I tried hitching north to Zinder but all the cars drove straight past me without stopping. This was very different to my experience in northern Nigeria. I gave in and got into a shared taxi called a *taxi brousse* (bush taxi) which stopped at a beautiful village en route. The road was paved as far as Zinder so this was one of the fastest drives for a long time.

I arrived in Zinder around midday and the *taxi brousse* stopped in a central square that was a cross between a lorry park and a market. It was very busy and very hot, in the high thirties. I was still wearing the clothes I had travelled through the Congo

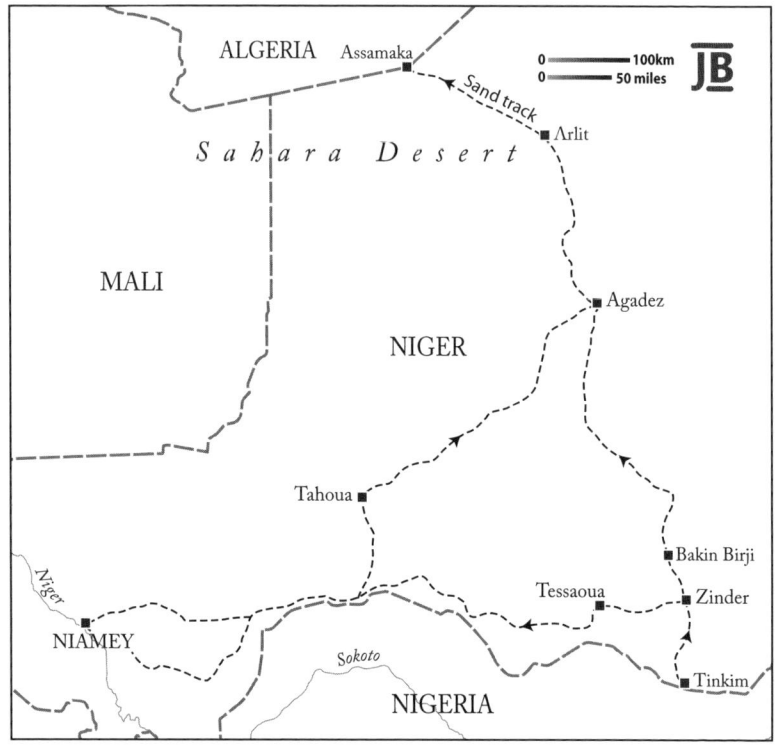

rainforest in and they were not suitable for this climate. Most men and women were wearing the long white robes called *djellabas*. I went to a stall that looked popular and tried one on. It was perfect for the weather, very light, the white cloth reflecting the heat of the sun, and each small breath of wind cooled me down. I bought two, reckoning I would wear them all the way back to Europe. And I did.

The tiny amount of Niger currency that I had changed at the border was just enough to buy the two *djellabas*. I saw a money-changing stall in the market and headed there. I had a talk with the stallholder and discussed the rate, which was good. We agreed a sum in exchange for my US dollars and as I went to get these out of my money pouch my bag of malaria pills fell out and some of the little white pills spilled onto the ground. I heard a voice shouting, 'Drugs!' I froze. I knew what that meant.

In no time at all there were at least 100 people gathered around me, grabbing me and shouting. I've never been more terrified in my life. I tried to explain to the people nearest to me that these were malaria pills, but the crowd was really worked up. I was crying by now and some of the men were hitting me.

In what seemed like no time at all I heard a siren and a police van appeared. The crowd parted and two policemen took me and my bag and bundled me into the van, driving off with the siren walling. The ride took less than 10 minutes and although I was relieved not to be in the aggressive crowd, I was absolutely terrified of what was to come.

I didn't have to wait long. We arrived at the police station and I was taken out, with each policeman holding one of my arms. I was taken into an office and stood in front of a table with a senior officer sitting behind. I was shaking with fear but also decided to try and calmly explain that this was a mistake. I started to do this in my best French and brought out the bag with the rest of my malaria pills. I attempted to reason with him but he grabbed the bag, picked out one of the pills and sniffed it, looking up at his colleagues and declaring, 'Drugs.'

This wasn't going well and I kept explaining as best as I could what these pills were and how it was all a big mix-up. Eventually the senior policeman told me to sit down and be quiet. I obeyed. He then picked up the telephone and dialled a number, and there followed a long phone call. I could not really make out what was being said but it was clearly complicated. After about half an hour, he put the phone down.

He then said, 'The inspector will decide what to do with you.'

'Where is the inspector?' I asked.

'He will come,' he replied and with that he waved me away. The two policemen took me outside where I could see a long single-storey brick building that had doors with bars across them. It was the cell block. I was ushered into one of the cells, and the barred door was shut and locked.

It was mid-afternoon. I was really terrified. I sat on the floor with my back against the wall trying to keep calm but it was hard. My head was full of terrifying thoughts. I suspected that the drug laws were very harsh for possession (you'd get 15 to 25 years today). I felt helpless, frightened, angry and very, very alone.

The sun started to set and a small plate of beans and rice was put under the bars of the door. I was hungry and ate the food. There was no furniture at all, just a bucket in the corner. I hoped I wouldn't need to use it. I had my bag with me but my passport and money had been taken from me, as well as the malaria pills. I slept fitfully and woke up many times with nightmares. I cried a lot. To this day this was the worst night of my life.

I woke in the morning and remembered that I had a note from my doctor in the UK prescribing the malaria pills. It was in English, but it was on official paper. I dug around in my bag and found it. Maybe this would help.

A policeman came to the door and pushed a tin mug of lukewarm black sugary tea under the bars of the door.

'Where is the inspector?' I asked as politely as I could muster.

He replied, 'He is coming,' which was of no use to me.

I sat in the corner of the cell feeling miserable for the next few hours and then I heard a loud discussion going on in the distance. It sounded heated.

Eventually two policemen came and opened the metal-barred door to the cell. I was escorted to the office where the discussion had been taking place. A tall, well-dressed police officer, who was clearly the inspector, was flanked by two of the officers who had sent me to the cell yesterday. But the atmosphere had changed. The inspector was all smiles and although the other two officers looked a little chastened, all was well. There was talk of 'an error' and a cup of tea produced. I must have stunk to high hell by now, and I looked a mess, but they ignored that.

After about half an hour of smiles and protestations of an unfortunate mistake, my bag was brought to me, my passport, money and pills were produced and I was offered a lift back into the town. When we got there a crowd gathered around, largely made up of the men who had grabbed and hit me the day before. But this time people were friendly and making jokes about yesterday. This was really hypocritical after their behaviour the previous day but I was left with a sense that most people were terrified of the police and now that I had been released it was necessary to make light of the event.

Most of all I felt incredibly lucky.

TRAVELLING NORTH

I wanted to get out of Zinder as soon as possible, hopefully never to return. I walked around the central square asking if any of the lorries were heading towards Agadez in the north, a journey of 280 miles. Eventually I found one that was prepared to take me. I climbed up and sat on the top of the lorry load, hanging on to the ropes as I had in Sudan. It was hot but out of reach of the crowd of men and after a while they dispersed.

After what felt like a long wait, the lorry set off. It was not too full on top, just eight of us. The road was rough, mostly compacted sand rutted where there had previously been rain. The lorry kept breaking down every few miles so it was a very slow journey. As evening arrived we came to the village of Bakin Birji, just 36 miles north of Zinder. The lorry stopped and I climbed down.

There was a small group of local people standing around and one of them came up to me.

'Welcome to our village,' he said. 'My name is Abu Bakr and I run a business here. You look very tired – would you like to come to my house?'

'Yes please,' I said, feeling pretty feeble at this point. I must have looked dreadful and this kind man saw how tired and dirty I was.

When we got to his house he gave me a bowl of warm water to wash, his wife cooked a beautiful meal of beans and flatbread, and then they offered me a bed for the night. I was tired and emotional and fought back tears as I accepted his family's generosity. In the morning Abu Bakr found me a lift on a different lorry. I gave the family a London postcard.

'There is a permit system for lorries and that lorry you arrived on yesterday had no such permit,' said Abu Bakr. He found me an altogether better lorry that didn't break down once on the remaining 204-mile drive to Agadez. We left around midday and it was a really beautiful journey. This was the Sahel, the region that stretches 3,670 miles from the Atlantic Ocean in the west to the Red Sea in the east, in a belt of between 200 to 600 miles wide, taking in many of the countries I had already passed through.

As the sun set, the full moon rose over an idyllic old village where we stopped for the night in a small lorry park. This was also an overnight stop for Tuareg people, the traditionally nomadic people who make up much of the population of the Sahara desert. Those we met that night were travelling with camels, and were dressed in blue cloaks with black headscarves. It was my first encounter with a people whom I would see a lot of over the next few weeks.

It was a couple of hours' drive the next morning to Agadez where I thanked my driver and went off to find out about the Algerian visa situation. I was keen to cross the Sahara to get to Algeria, which I had been told by travellers was the best and most exciting route. I had also heard that Algeria, having recently gained a new moderate president, was a great country to travel through. But the visa requirements for backpackers were somewhat opaque.

Agadez was a beautiful city with a population of 130,000 in 1980. Most of the typically two-storey buildings were made from the traditional mud brick of the Sahel and were laid out in a grid pattern. There were a few trees on the streets and the town was surrounded on all sides by the south of the Sahara Desert with many people, mostly refugees, living in tents. I had never heard of Agadez before my journey and was stunned by its ancient beauty.

I found a hotel just opposite the main mosque (which, at 87 feet tall, is still the tallest mud-brick building in the world). There were a few backpackers sitting in a bar that of course didn't sell alcohol. I spoke to one of them, who told me that they allowed backpackers to sleep on the roof for a very small fee. I sat in the bar and asked what people knew about visas. There were lots of stories but the general consensus was that as a Brit I could get a visa but would need to go to the Algerian Embassy in Niamey, the capital. My heart sank. Niamey was 570 miles away on the most direct route, but most of the lorries went via Zinder which was 800 miles.

I was pretty tired by now. I hadn't really recovered from the anxiety and terror of my arrest and night in a jail cell. I spent most of the rest of the day discussing options with the backpackers – this was clearly a discussion held most days, especially when a new traveller arrived. The main story was of a group of travellers from the Netherlands known as 'The Dutch at In Guezzam'. They were travelling in a vehicle and had assumed that they could cross the border from Niger to Algeria at the southern Algerian town of In Guezzam. Once they had arrived at the Algerian border post they were told that they could not enter Algeria as they had no visas, but having already crossed the border illegally, they were told that they could not travel back to Niger. Some days had passed and according to the story there were telegrams sent to the Netherlands embassies in Algiers (capital of Algeria) and Niamey (capital of Niger) as well as the Ministry of Foreign Affairs of The Netherlands. After some time the compromise was reached that one of their party could travel to Niamey to hopefully obtain visas for the whole group, taking all their passports with him. As far as anyone knew the remainder were still waiting at In Guezzam, camping on the outskirts of this town, temporarily stateless.

I'd been travelling for a while and was well aware that travellers' tales are often as tall as a story can get. Nonetheless, I did not fancy becoming stateless myself. I went to sleep on the hotel roof that night, watching the stars and hoping for inspiration in the morning. I woke as the sun rose and knew what to do. But I was really tired at this point and just needed a day's rest. I decided to have that and take it easy. I walked around Agadez a little and otherwise relaxed in the hotel and went to sleep again on the roof watching the sky full of stars.

1,400-MILE DETOUR

The next morning I went down to the lorry park early and quickly got a lift on a lorry going back to Zinder. I felt uncomfortable going back there but could not risk crossing the border to Algeria without a visa. I felt a bit stupid going back the way I had come but got over that quickly. I was feeling a bit stuck in a country that I wasn't enjoying as much as the others I had travelled through. I was generally struggling with food, as it was a very meat-orientated diet. I was mostly living on gravy and flatbread, with the occasional plate of beans. I was run-down and now I was heading off across the country in pursuit of a visa. And I was still feeling anxious following the night I had spent in jail in Zinder.

It was a long eight-hour drive to Zinder and here I was back in the same *autogare* where I was welcomed back as a sort of local hero as if I had escaped years of incarceration. I personally could have done without the attention but had no choice. And yet again I had some form of trouble at Zinder, this time changing US dollars to CFA francs, the currency of Niger. The bank refused to do this for me and I was forced to change with a black-market trader, which I was nervous about, concerned about the risk of arrest. But I had no choice as I had no local currency left. All was well and I got a better rate than the bank offered.

It was late afternoon with just a couple of hours of sunlight left and I decided to take a Toyota shared minibus, which was more comfortable and drove faster than a lorry. It did mean paying, however, which I did not have to do on lorries. Yet again it was largely a dusty road, with occasional sections of tarmac in some of the towns. The minibus stopped at all of the towns and many of the villages, dropping off and collecting people. Sometimes it was very crowded and other times it felt more spacious. To call it a minibus was perhaps a bit grand – it was really a small pickup truck with bench seating on either side and a canopy over the top to keep off the direct sunlight. The flapping of the canopy created enough wind to keep us cooler, but when we stopped I could feel the temperature, which was well over 35 degrees.

We stopped the night at the small town of Tessaoua. The drive from Tessaoua to Niamey the next day took 12 hours and we arrived around 7pm. The ride had been bumpy, I had been bitten by mosquitos in the night and I had a bad heat blister on one of my shoulders. Hugo and Antoine were two French travellers on the same minibus and we all shared a room in the Domino Hotel, conveniently near the Algerian Embassy. I had a mint tea in a bar with a local man named Moies who was very interesting.

'Niger is a police state,' he said. 'They can do pretty much what they want.' I decided not to mention my recent experience of this.

I was down at the Algerian Embassy first thing in the morning. After completing the forms, I showed them my passport which they photocopied and let me have back. This was a big relief as I hated having to leave my passport at an embassy, which I had had to do quite a bit. While I was sitting in the waiting area I got into a conversation with Thomas, who turned out to be the member of the 'Dutch at In Guezzam' group who had taken all the passports to Niamey to get visas for them all.

'It is very frustrating, as I feel like I'm being messed about,' he said. 'The embassy staff have made me wait two weeks so far saying they will be ready tomorrow.'

'I wish there was something I could do,' I said.

'Let me show you around the city. That will take my mind off it all,' Thomas replied.

Hugo and Antoine were staying for a few days before heading west and with Thomas as our guide we spent the rest of the day exploring the city, of which by now he was an expert. He took us to great food stalls where I ate beans and macaroni in a lovely sauce and drank fabulous coffee. The food was better than I had eaten in a long time and as always that cheered me up. And it was good to have a day off the road. I spoke with them about my experience of being jailed for a night in Zinder. It was good to talk about it and they were all very sympathetic.

Late that afternoon I went back to the Algerian Embassy and the visa was ready. My passport was stamped and I could enter the country. All very exciting, and I realised how much I had wanted to get to Algeria.

'I feel embarrassed that I have got my visa so quickly,' I told Thomas.

'Don't be ridiculous,' he replied. 'And anyway you can take a letter to my friends at In Guezzam.' Thomas had already written a lengthy letter and I promised to take it to them as soon as I could get there. 'That will be sooner than me,' he said.

The next morning I checked out of the hotel. I went to the *autogare* and found a bus heading to Tahoua which would be the quickest route back to Agadez. I got on the bus and was glad I wasn't riding on the top of a lorry as rain poured down for most of the journey. It was a long drive – nine hours with stops – and there wasn't any food available, so I was very hungry when I arrived at the outskirts of Tahoua.

We stopped at a police roadblock on the edge of the town, which was not unusual. But this time the police insisted that everyone got out of the bus, bringing their luggage for a search. And sure enough they unpacked my bag, found my malaria pills and started talking about drugs. This time I stayed calm, brought out my valuable prescription from the UK and explained in my best French that these were pills for malaria. Thankfully on this occasion the police saw sense and I was waved back on to the bus. Niger was definitely a police state and getting in and out of towns was not always easy. I found a small café in the centre of Tahoua where I ate an enormous bowl of beans and gravy. Farooq, the owner, took pity on me and showed me to a mattress in the storeroom where I slept the night.

I woke the next morning refreshed and had a cup of *shi* with Farooq. His English was about as good as my French, which had got a lot better by now.

'I am very happy with my café, we are doing so well and my family are very proud of me,' he said. 'But what are you doing here in my town?'

I briefly told him about my journey, that I had left university and wanted to travel before I got a job.

'You have been to university,' he said, 'and yet you are travelling on a bus. I would expect you to have a Land Rover.'

Farooq was interesting and our conversation went on until mid-morning, broken up by customers coming in for a drink and a snack. I thanked him, giving him one of the postcards, and wandered down to the *autogare* where I met Chloé, Juliette and

Pierre, French backpackers waiting for transport to Agadez. I joined them and about an hour later a *taxi brousse* arrived with seating for all four of us, heading to Agadez. While we were waiting I met a traveller who was heading to Niamey from Agadez.

'I met your friend Rob in Agadez two days ago,' he said. 'He has been asking everyone and I recognised you immediately from his description.'

'Do you know where he's heading now?' I asked.

'He said that he is heading north to Tamanrasset in Algeria.'

I felt a pang of sadness at missing Rob again and hoped that he might be delayed in Agadez waiting for a lift.

It was an eight-hour drive to Agadez with three short stops. Luckily I had bought a large takeaway meal from Farooq's café and shared it with my fellow travellers. The road was bumpy, dusty and mostly empty, with just a few villages along the way. It was nearly 10pm when we arrived, heading straight to the hotel I had stayed in only five nights before. Despite the late hour the manager rustled up some food for us and we joined the few travellers in the bar that didn't sell alcohol. And then we all went up to the roof to sleep.

AGADEZ

I spent the next five days in Agadez waiting for transport north across the Sahara to Algeria. I wasn't alone. There were maybe 10 other travellers waiting for the same thing, all of them in small groups. Every morning and evening the backpackers would go down to the *autogare* on the edge of the town to see whether any of the lorry drivers there would take passengers. A few left each day, but it transpired that the best way to get a lift was with a driver in a private vehicle who needed a companion. The bulk of the journey was on sand, parts of which were soft, so it was far too dangerous to drive alone. That possibility only really worked for solo travellers, putting me at an advantage.

My first morning I went with some of the travellers to the *autogare*. There were only a handful of lorries so I left the others, betting on finding a solo car driver who wanted company.

Quite a few people had seen Rob, who had clearly given my description to everyone. Just as well I wasn't on the run from the police. He had left the day before I arrived. So I had overtaken him somewhere between Cameroon and Niger, and then fallen behind again. By now I was missing my travelling companion. I was hoping to see him again, but I had to accept that this might not happen.

The hotel was in the centre of the town, very close to the Agadez Mosque. Its name was Auberge Tellit Rafael Antunes and there was a great view of the mosque from the roof where I was sleeping. There weren't many visitors staying there so the hotel encouraged backpackers to stay on the roof, I imagine earning some money largely from the food and drink that we bought. It was where all the backpackers stayed and hung out waiting for transport and so would be the best place for me to meet a solo driver looking for a companion. I spent a lot of time in and around the hotel, mostly drinking *emu-hari*, a sweet lemony-gingery drink.

There was lots to see in Agadez. Almost all the buildings were built of red clay and the streets were narrow, so there were few vehicles in the centre of the town. There were cafés, shops, markets and lots to explore. My favourite was the Animal Market. On my second morning I went to this market just outside the town in the desert. Most of the men were Tuareg dressed in blue and white with large, mostly black, headscarves. They sat on the ground surrounded by their camels, donkeys and goats.

The camel drivers arrived with their camels in groups, swords hanging around their shoulders and some of their animals wearing brightly coloured saddles. It was a scene that cannot have changed for centuries. There was plenty of haggling over the price of a goat, donkey and occasionally a camel, all carried out in a very relaxed and friendly manner. I watched a long train of maybe 12 camels arrive, with Tuareg traders riding three of them and the rest laden with all manner of goods – mostly large cardboard boxes containing televisions and other electrical items tied on to the animals' backs and sides. I was intrigued.

The camel train came to a halt and the camels went down on their knees and eventually sat on the sand. The men dismounted and squatted by their beasts or found some shade to sit in, rolling out straw mats. Despite their swords, I plucked up the courage to talk to the group of camel drivers that had just arrived. They spoke little French and no English, but I had learned a smattering of words in Arabic from my time in Egypt and Sudan. After plenty of greetings such as 'salam-u-laikum' (peace be with you) I asked about the televisions. These were destined to be sold to wealthy households in Libya. It would take them at least 25 days' travel across the Sahara Desert, a long journey, but the trade was lucrative and well worth it, a perfect profession for a nomadic people.

As well as the trade in animals that was taking place there were tents clustered where older men squatted and read beautifully scripted books in Arabic, written in red and black ink. Women and girls sold a soft goat's cheese and little biscuits to eat it on. I hadn't eaten much cheese for a while and this was delicious. They were also selling all types of purses, wallets, saddles for camels, straw hats, jewellery, clothing, rugs and more. All the vendors were Tuareg.

I had a browse around the stalls and decided to buy a few gifts for my family. I watched a Tuareg family arriving from the desert on camels and donkeys. The women were sitting astride their animals, on top of piles of rugs, gourds filled with liquids and sacks of goods to sell. Children rode on the donkeys. Camels relaxed with their necks outstretched and heads lying forward flat on the ground.

On my fifth day in Agadez I spent a couple of hours at the hotel in the morning waiting for a driver to appear, then went for a walk in the town. I found one of the markets and ate lunch, bread and gravy as always. This was pretty much all that was available for a vegetarian. I was looking forward to eating vegetables and fruit again. By early afternoon, when it was over 40 degrees, I went back in the hotel. There were a few French travellers still there, a group of three men and a married couple having the honeymoon of a lifetime. That evening some of us went to see a band of local musicians.

When we got back to the hotel there was a new French traveller there. He came up to me immediately.

'Hello Patrick, my name is Claude. I hear you want a lift across the desert.'

'Yes please, I would love that,' I quickly replied. 'But how did you know my name?'

'All the travellers here told me about you. I only have room for one companion in my little red Renault Four.'

We carried on talking late about the journey ahead until I headed upstairs for my final night on the roof of the hotel, falling asleep beneath another sky speckled white with stars.

SAHARA

Claude and I ate breakfast in the hotel early.

'Why are you driving across the desert?' I asked.

'I've always wanted to drive across the Sahara,' he said. 'I've taken an extended break from my work. I flew to Amsterdam a week and a half ago and then got a flight to Kano. I bought the car and equipment and then drove here to Agadez. I knew that I would need to find a companion for the drive to Tamanrasset but was sure I would find someone and here you are.'

'What will you do after Tamanrasset?' I asked.

'I would have liked to drive through Morocco and back to Paris,' he replied, 'but the border is closed, at least to drivers. So I will drive to Algiers and get a ferry to Marseille. How did you get here?'

'That's a very long story, but we will have lots of time on the drive for me to tell you,' I replied.

We went to his car, which was full of his luggage plus four large jerrycans that took up all of the back seat area, where the seats had been removed. There was just enough room for my tiny bag. We headed to the only petrol station in town and filled two cans with petrol and two with water. It looked like a lot but we would need these for the 540-mile drive to Tamanrasset, most of which would be over sand and much of that soft.

We went to the market and bought food for the long journey. We could not assume that we would make the trip quickly – we could get stuck in the sand or the car could break down. Claude reckoned that if all went well we could make it to Tamanrasset in three or maybe four days if we had trouble with the car. We bought food for seven days just to be sure. That said, there wasn't a great choice of what we could buy as he only had a small gas camping stove, one saucepan and no refrigerator.

By 9.30 we were ready to go and drove out of the town. The first four and a half hours to the town of Arlit was an easy drive on tarmac. Arlit is a town that services Niger's uranium mines, hence the tarmac road. Niger has Africa's highest-grade uranium, producing over 2,000 tonnes of uranium in 2022, about 5% of the world's mining output. Most of this comes from the two mines near Arlit.

On either side of the tarmac road the countryside was barren but after Arlit we were suddenly in the desert. There was no more road, just a few tyre trails in the sand to mark the direction we should be travelling in. Every kilometre was, apparently, marked by a large wooden stake to indicate that drivers were heading the right way. Within 15 miles of Arlit the car had two punctures and we had to stop to fix them. It became quickly clear how much Claude needed a passenger as it took the two of us to fix these punctures.

'Your most important job is to look out for soft sand,' said Claude. 'You look for any slight change in colour which might indicate that it is soft.'

So I would spend the rest of the journey to Tamanrasset looking intently out of the front windscreen. There were small dunes around and it was best to avoid the base of these, where the sand was softest.

'Shout out "Soft Sand!" when you see a change in the colour or texture of the sand,' he said. 'I would rather you called a false alarm than the car gets stuck.'

At first I called out 'Soft Sand!' too often but in no time I got the hang of it. So mostly the sand was soft when I called it. Claude would stop the car, we would both get out and walk to the area that

I thought was soft. If I was wrong, we would get back in the car and drive on.

But when I was right, the routine could take a long time. We would empty the car of everything, jerrycans of fuel and water, food and luggage, and start carrying it across the soft sand until we felt the sand become hard underfoot. Then we would leave what we had carried and go back for more. Sometimes the patch of soft sand could take 20 to 30 minutes to walk across, sometimes more like 5 minutes. It would take two trips for us both to carry our large cans of petrol and water as well as the bags of food. Once back at the almost empty car, I would carry our personal baggage, walk across the soft sand and stand about 15 feet beyond the edge of the hard sand.

Meanwhile Claude would reverse the car some 40 feet, then drive very fast towards the start of the soft sand and carry on towards me at the same speed. It was brilliant – the car glided over the soft sand and came to a halt near to where I was standing. I would congratulate him and then we would load up the car again and carry on.

The temperature got really hot during the day – typically around 38 degrees but sometimes well over 40 degrees in the middle of the day. Driving helped cool us down a bit but even with the windows open it was very hot. When we stopped, mostly to do the soft sand routine, white insects that looked like mosquitos swarmed around our heads and sometimes bit.

'They won't give us malaria,' said Claude.

'Just as well, because I've already had malaria twice on this journey,' I said and then proceeded to tell him of the night on the River Congo and how Michael and his family had looked after me.

Mid-afternoon on the first day we came across an Algerian driver who had broken down. We stopped and I got out. 'Do you need any help?' I asked in my best Arabic.

'Yes please,' he said in perfect English. 'I have just changed one of the tyres and now I can't start the engine.'

Claude looked at the driver's engine and fiddled around with the spark plugs, and after a few more attempts the engine started. He was thrilled. He was heading to Arlit for the night, which we were confident he could make as long as he didn't have to stop the car.

We set off and half an hour later we got stuck. I had spotted some soft sand and we had gone through the routine again. We had loaded the car back up and then about 100 feet from the beginning of the hard sand we hit another patch of soft sand which I hadn't spotted.

'It's inevitable that this would happen at least once,' Claude said generously.

We stopped and Claude got out his two ramps, each nearly two feet long.

'You are really well prepared,' I commented.

I then used his folding shovel to dig, creating a packed path of hard sand that extended at least six feet in front of each tyre. While I was doing this, Claude cleared the sand away from beneath the underside of the vehicle. 'The less sand that's touching the vehicle, the less resistance there will be,' he explained.

I then put a ramp on to each path and pushed them each underneath the tires. Then it was time for Claude to try and drive out. He drove on to the ramps and up the paths I had created but once the car was out of this it got stuck in the sand again. After a shout of 'Damn', we redid the whole routine. We carried on like this for an hour, moving a few feet each time. Eventually Claude drove the car on to the hard sand.

By now the sun was setting and the temperature dropping. Both fell fast and so it was time to stop for the night. We cooked some tinned beans on the gas stove, wrapped up warm and sat watching the huge numbers of stars that filled the sky. Later we slept in the car. It wasn't as cold at night as I had expected and we both managed to sleep well after our exertions.

The next day we woke before the sun came up, brewed up some black tea with sugar, ate some flatbread and set off again. We drove across flat, sandy desert, interrupted every hour or so with a patch of soft sand we had to negotiate. Although there were many of these they were mostly short in length and we were getting quicker at our routine.

The desert was really stunning. The orange and yellow sand stretched as far as I could see in all directions. There were a few dunes visible far away on the horizon. By mid-morning we arrived at the Niger border post at the small town of Assamaka. The border post was a small orange mud building with sand piled up against the wall on one side. There was a small sign saying 'Poste Frontalier Assamaka' where we stopped to show our passports. We waited for a while. Once they were stamped we headed off to In Guezzam and Algeria which took about an hour. I felt sorry for the two border guards who lived in a tent next to this old, decrepit building, a pretty remote and lonely place.

In 2023 a military coup removed the elected President of Niger. The new military-led government expelled the French troops who had been there for many years. In 2024 an agreement was reached with Russia, with Russian military trainers and equipment arriving in Niger. As of 2024, the country is the sixth-poorest in the world[21].

---

21   ⊘ gfmag.com/data/economic-data/poorest-country-in-the-world

8

ALGERIA

SAHARA

I was always excited crossing the border to another country: a mix of anticipation of the new and anxiety about what the customs and immigration welcome would be like. On this occasion arriving in Algeria was quite dramatic.

We passed through Niger customs at Assamaka and headed across the sand the 18 miles to In Guezzam, where the Algerian border was located. As usual I was looking out for soft sand and as we drove up to the customs post shouted, 'Soft Sand!' It was too late, the car ground to a halt and we were stuck.

As we got out of the car to start the process of digging it out, four Algerian soldiers emerged from the building, one of them carrying a superior spade. 'Welcome to Algeria!' they shouted, laughing at our predicament.

In no time they had dug a trench and Claude drove out of the sand and up to their small building. Just as well, as the temperature was over 40 degrees. The soldiers were very friendly, bringing us coffee while they stamped our passports. They even had a mud-built swimming pool at the back and encouraged us to stop for a dip. We needed no encouragement and were soon cooling down in the water. To this day it's my best-ever welcome to a country.

When we finished our swim we drove up to where the famous 'Dutch at In Guezzam' were camping. 'I have a letter from Thomas,' I called out from the car. They all jumped up and cheered. While they heated their stove to brew some coffee there was silence as

they gathered around and read the letter. If they were disappointed about the long wait they didn't show it.

'How is Thomas doing?' one of them asked.

'He is really impressive,' I said. 'He seems to be able to remain positive despite the endless delays.'

They liked that and then told us a little about how life was here. 'The Algerian border guards are lovely, they provide food and water and let us use the swimming pool. They are very friendly and embarrassed about what they call "typical bureaucracy" that is slowing up our getting visas.'

We had been talking for a while when one of them said, 'Your friend Rob passed through six days ago and said he plans to wait a while for you at Tamanrasset.' That was exciting news. We shared some food with the Dutch and then after farewells and good-luck wishes, Claude and I were on our way. I later heard that after a wait of nearly six weeks they got their visas and travelled home via Algeria and Morocco.

We drove on across the sand and in the next 60 miles we stopped for soft sand five times and saw just one other vehicle in the distance. At one point we thought we had missed the one-kilometre marker pole. Claude stopped the car, got out a map and compass and after discussion we headed off in the direction that we both thought made sense. We had an anxious twenty minutes but eventually we saw a marker post looming on the horizon, like a lighthouse on the ocean. We cheered.

That evening we saw our first massive sand dune, along with some incredible rock formations. We stopped the car and watched the sun set over the dune, one of the many beautiful sights of my journey. 'This is where I miss having my camera,' I said. Claude got out his camera and took some pictures, but as it was many years before digital photography I never got to see them.

We stopped for the night, cooking beans from a tin and wrapping up warm to watch the stars before sleeping. We woke a couple of hours later to the sound of wind and got into the car quickly before being enveloped by a sandstorm that carried on for the rest of the night.

This was very different to the travelling I had been doing for the last few months. We saw hardly anyone, it was just the two of us alone. Walking in the Congo rainforest and travelling on lorries in Sudan, there were always plenty of people to share the experience. The Sahara was an empty place.

Next morning we woke up in the car, stiff and having had a poor night's sleep. There was sand on the dashboard and every surface. There was sand in our clothes, our hair, ears and noses. We got out and shook ourselves down, wiping the worst of it off the seats and out of the car. We drank some water, ate some biscuits and headed off into the desert, looking out for the next marker post and focussing on spotting soft sand.

We had a few patches of soft sand in the morning and twice had to unload the car, getting more sand out from last night's storm each time. Around midday we began to see the jagged peaks of the Hoggar Mountains, a large highland region in the centre of the Sahara. We passed through a couple of *oueds* (wadis) – ravines or channels that are dry except in the rainy season. These weren't inhabited but there were a few plants and even some fruit, a rare sight in the desert. We stopped at the second *oued* and got out of the car to have a look. As we returned to the car it suddenly rained very hard for five minutes. We stood outside, as it was blissful to feel wet.

COUSCOUS

Later that afternoon we arrived at Tamanrasset. We drove to the Post Office where I went to the Poste Restante and collected two letters from home. Then we found a campsite on the edge of the town and parked up for the night. Along the roadside there were lots of street food vendors and the smell was delicious. I went up to one and asked, 'Is there meat in this?'

The cook laughed and said, 'Of course not.'

Vegetarian food was really easy to come by in Algeria. That evening Claude and I sat by the side of the road eating couscous with tomatoes, courgettes, chickpeas, dried apricots, dates and herbs. I had never eaten couscous before and have been a lifelong fan ever since. After a huge plate we were offered a fresh mint tea with *msemen*, a flat, square-shaped pancake that our chef cooked in a pan over the hot coals and finished off with a mix of butter, honey and rose water. This was without doubt the most delicious meal I had eaten since Egypt, cooked right in front of us on the side of the road. After 45 years I can still remember the delight I had eating this food.

Claude and I were sitting around the chef with a group of travellers who were staying in the campsite. Most of them were travelling in Morocco and Algeria and Tamanrasset was the furthest south they would be going on their travels. 'Have any of you met Rob?' I asked, giving a description of him.

'Yes, we have,' said a woman and her partner. 'He left two days ago, heading to In Salah.'

I was excited. 'Is he still hoping to meet up with me?' I asked. They replied that he had been asking quite a few people to look out for me.

We had a slow start the next day before leaving Tamanrasset. The road was now tarmac, but it was often hidden by drifting sands so we could still get stuck if we accidentally went off the road. We stopped for a while in the mountains. Some of these looked more like cathedrals or castles. Sometimes it was hard to tell whether they were mountains or sand dunes. It was an absolutely stunning sight. We stopped for a break near Arak when there was a massive rainstorm which lasted about 20 minutes. This time we stopped and stayed in the car until the rain passed. I hadn't expected rain in the desert like this.

It was dark when we drove into In Salah. Like most towns in Algeria, In Salah had a campsite where travellers stayed alongside Tuareg camel trains. We stopped at the site and I looked for travellers; in no time I found a few sitting around a food stall eating couscous. And yes, they had met Rob, but they weren't sure where he was heading. One thought that he was taking the route from In Salah west via the town of Reggane. We joined this group and had another delicious meal of vegetable couscous. I felt so good after eating this food, realising that I hadn't been eating well for many months now, partly because there was often not much food available but mostly because most of what was available was meat. Travelling in Africa as a vegetarian had been very challenging.

We drove north in the morning after brewing a cup of tea and watching the sun rise over the mountains. Very occasionally we would see another vehicle. Claude and I chatted about all sorts of things, mostly telling our stories of what we had experienced in our respective Africa trips as well as marvelling at the sights we were seeing now. Every so often we would see a camel train led by Tuareg in the distance. They stayed away from the road. A couple of times there was a small sandstorm and we stopped the car and shut all the windows for 10 to 15 minutes while it blew through.

Claude was keen to crack on as he had a deadline for a ferry in Algiers and I was keen to meet with Rob again. We carried on through beautiful landscapes of sand dunes and occasional mountains and rock formations. I had hoped to have met Rob at El Golea but the information from the night before was that he had travelled in a different direction. I was sad but resigned to travelling alone after leaving Claude. I could have continued with him to Algiers but was keen to see more of Algeria and travel through Morocco. I felt my journey would be incomplete without spending time in these two countries.

REUNION

We drove into El Golea late afternoon after crossing a long plateau with high sand dunes dotted across the otherwise flat landscape. As usual we drove into the campsite, and who should be sitting around a food stall with a group of travellers but Rob. It was a real surprise as I had assumed that the information I'd been given was correct and that he had travelled across Algeria by a different route.

He jumped up and I leapt out of the car and we gave each other a massive hug. He was as pleased to see me as I was him. 'I assume this is Rob,' said Claude and I introduced them both.

The three of us sat together while we ate a plate of couscous. Rob and I could barely contain ourselves with our stories as we both wanted to know what had happened to the other since we parted company in Bangui, 3,460 miles and some time ago.

Then Rob asked, 'Did you get malaria?'

I nodded.

'When you didn't appear at Ngaoundéré I remembered the night on the Congo. How was it?'

'It was pretty bad and I'm still weaker than I was before,' I said. 'But I experienced the most extraordinary kindness from Michael, the local Director of UNICEF, and his family. Without his support I expect I would have been much more ill or worse.' I was sombre as I said this; it was the first time I had properly acknowledged that possibility. Claude and Rob caught the moment.

We talked late into the night. It was lovely and the two of them got on well. Claude had of course heard all my stories and was sometimes telling Rob what had happened to me, which was really funny. He was clearly taken with both of our adventures. Towards the end of the evening, Claude broached the subject that we had avoided so far. 'It's time for you two to travel together again. I will leave you tomorrow and wish you both well.'

I welled up with tears. The two of us hugged. I had really enjoyed the journey with Claude and his little red Renault that had served us well across the sand. Claude left in the morning with Rob and me waving him off.

Before our reunion, Rob had found a lift to Timimoun with some Germans but there was no room for another passenger. 'No problem, I'll hitch a ride,' I said.

'I'll wait for you at Timimoun, even if you take a month,' he replied.

After breakfast, I walked to the road at the edge of town and started putting out my hand at each vehicle that would come past. The problem was that there was almost no traffic. I didn't worry as I was soon joined by Omar, who was a little older than me. By now my French was passable so we were able to talk and I learned quite a lot about Algeria.

'I am very proud to be Algerian,' he said. 'The government is socialist in deed as well as in name. The economy is strong, largely because we have oil reserves, but the money is shared.'

'How is it shared?' I asked.

'There are lots of examples,' he continued. 'Healthcare is free. The government funds free machinery and working cash for farmers. And every town has a *Jardin* with oranges and dates that are free for all to pick, even travellers.'

Omar asked me a lot about life in the UK and was particularly interested in whether I had been to Paris. Many of the younger Algerians I met wanted to move to Paris, seeing it as a place they could make money and become successful.

Late morning a car came by hooting its horn. Omar and I got very excited, thinking this would be a lift for one or both of us. But it turned out to be Rob with his German friends. We waved and carried on waiting. From time to time children would appear and shout '*Ajnabiun!*', meaning 'Foreigner'. They were generally quite friendly and unusually didn't ask for money. Although one boy appeared with my sunglasses. His father followed behind him and started beating him about badly so I intervened asking Omar to explain that I had lost them. The father stopped and was friendly. I had no idea whether the boy had found the sunglasses or stolen them but was upset about the brutality of the father. Half an hour later a woman appeared with a plate of couscous, beans, lentils, vegetables and meat for Omar and me to share (he ate the meat). This was probably related to the sunglasses incident.

After lunch Omar said, 'I can see a bus coming – let's get a ride on this.'

I agreed as it was very hot and I was keen to catch up with Rob. We hailed the bus, which stopped, and the fare to Timimoun was cheap. This was a lot of fun as Omar engaged me in a conversation with a group of young Algerians in a mixture of French and

English, falling into Arabic from time to time, which I struggled to understand despite having some words. We had a long talk about marriage which moved into the role of women and their subservience to men, particularly when married.

I had been cautious about being challenging elsewhere in my travels but somehow I felt free to challenge this here and I was surprised about the openness of our conversation. We also discussed food quotas, as it appears that only a certain amount of food can be sold by each shop and then sales must stop. This is even if there is more food remaining in the store, including perishables. 'This makes no sense,' I said. 'Can you explain why?'

'Bureaucracy,' they replied.

As the sun fell it lit up the mountains and sand into gold, orange and sometimes red. All conversation in the bus stopped as everyone looked out of the windows. We arrived in Timimoun in darkness after a four-and-a-half-hour drive through desert with occasional mountains and sand dunes. We sat in the square in the middle of the town listening to music played on the *mandole*, an instrument a bit like a long mandolin. Eventually Omar and I fell asleep on the street, along with some of the men from the bus. This seemed acceptable here.

SAND DUNES AND PALMS

The next morning Omar and I went to the nearest café and there was Rob. He had been looking for me. I said goodbye to Omar who was heading to the bus station to travel further.

'Let's walk to the *Palmeraie*,' said Rob, and we walked to the desert on the edge of the town, with sand dunes stretching beyond for miles. Here we found the *Palmeraie*, a huge palm grove that runs alongside Timimoun. We climbed a little way up one of the dunes, which was not easy, as our feet sank deep into the sand with each step. And the heat was close to 40 degrees. But it was worth it for the stunning view back over the oasis of palms that is Timimoun, surrounded by desert and dunes on all sides. We walked back through the *Palmeraie*, enjoying the irrigation channels feeding crops of maize and lots of dates. We walked around this beautiful little town of red ochre houses, narrow streets, small doors, shops and a market. It was like being in Lamu again, but red instead of white. That evening we slept out under our mosquito nets in the *Palmeraie*, after a meal of couscous and vegetables followed by dates.

The next morning we hitched a lift with a driver of a small pickup truck. We sat in the back and bounced up and down sitting on our small rucksacks, hoping we wouldn't damage ourselves. It was quite an ordeal and reminded me of some of the days on the top of the lorries in Sudan. The trip took five hours with a short break along the way at Ksabi, a tiny oasis village.

But it was worth it as Beni Abbes was simply one of the most beautiful places I have ever visited. It is called the 'Pearl of the Saoura'. The town was of red ochre and white buildings dwarfed by one of the largest sand dunes I had seen. In the centre of the town was the *Jardin*, the municipal swimming pool, shaded by date palms and cypress trees. We immediately went for a swim in the fresh cold water, which was heaven. The pool was decorative with tiled walls, a stone diving tower, changing rooms and shade. We had a conversation with the man on the gate who said we could stay each night for 50 dinar for the two of us, sleeping outside by the pool. We could not believe this. Fifty dinar was the equivalent of 10 pence in UK currency.

We immediately paid for two nights, walked into town and had a hot meal of couscous and vegetables in the market, then purchased dried fruit, nuts and bread to keep us going that evening. We spent the rest of the day swimming, resting and talking with the local young men who came down to swim that evening. They showed us how to suck fresh dates off the trees so that you left the stone still on its twig. It was a heavenly place to stay.

I had been fascinated by the sand dunes of the Sahara since first seeing them. 'For some reason I want to climb the dune and roll down it,' I said. 'I know it's a crazy idea but if I don't do this now I might never have the chance again.'

If Rob was surprised he didn't show it, saying, 'Let's do it.' We talked a bit about how we would manage this. We both had light, loose cotton trousers and light *djellabas* as well as long scarves of the type worn in Palestine and Egypt. We agreed that we would need to be fully clothed with the scarves wrapped tightly around our heads. We would not be able to see directly because of the risk of getting sand in our eyes but would be able to see a little through the scarves.

We set off with our water bottles full and climbed about 300 feet up to the top of the tallest of the dunes. Deciding that we would do it one at a time, I lay down on my side, held on to my water bottle and started to roll. I didn't move at all. So Rob pushed me and eventually I gained some momentum and started to roll down. Immediately sand flew everywhere and I shut my eyes and gave in to the experience of rolling. It was an extraordinary feeling, like a combination of dizziness and weightlessness.

Eventually I came to a halt, took off my scarf and looked back up the dune, feeling dizzy. I had rolled down about two thirds of it. I stood up and shook out what felt like a few sacks of sand that had gathered inside my clothes, my hair, nostrils and ears. Luckily I had kept my eyes shut. Rob let out a cheer from the top and proceeded to try and do it himself. He couldn't, so I climbed up and pushed him, telling him to keep his eyes shut. He rolled down as far as I had, while I jumped down a large step at a time, rather like moonwalking. It was a great experience but neither of us felt the need to repeat it, so we made our way back down the dune into the town and back to the *Jardin*, where we were in great need of a wash and a swim.

The next day we walked 10 miles out of Beni Abbes along the main road, which was almost empty. It was exhausting but I was really pleased that I could still walk this far despite the malaria I'd had in CAR. Around midday we got a lift from a driver who took us on to Béchar, a larger town which was quite industrial. We saw shops with lots of modern goods, hip Algerians and women dressed in Western styles, quite different to what we had seen elsewhere in the country. There was fruit to eat, including peaches and melons, which neither of us had tasted for a very long time.

BORDER TRICKS

We found a café and spent the afternoon forging our currency forms. I had been given a form when I entered Algeria at In Guezzam, which was to be filled in to demonstrate that I was spending the equivalent of US$25 a day while staying in the country. That sum sounds like nothing these days but I had been spending much less, closer to one or two dollars a day. So I had to forge signatures that showed I had exchanged currency. I was pleased with the job I had done and Rob was impressed enough to ask me to forge his. Only when we crossed the border would we discover if I was really any good and could make a career as a forger when I returned home.

That evening we hitched a ride with some men who took us to Beni Ounif and gave us dinner at the local hotel where we were also put up for the night. I ate a salad with olives. Olives! That was a taste I hadn't had for a long time. I was beginning to enjoy food again. Algeria was one of my favourite countries of the journey. I liked the enthusiasm and generosity of the people that I met. Although I think the delicious vegetarian food had something to do with it too.

Rob and I woke early and headed for the border. We had heard conflicting reports as to whether it would be open, but we decided to go for it anyway. We set off walking early to avoid the heat of the day, as it was a five-mile walk to Figuig, the Moroccan border town. We got to the Algerian border post in just over an hour and thankfully there was no problem with the currency declarations. In fact the customs officer didn't really look at them, he just seemed happy that we had them. Passports were stamped and we were told that it was reasonably likely that the Moroccan border guards would let us enter. We were a bit concerned about their use of the word 'reasonably' but we could see the border post in the distance and set off in what was now a 35-degree heat. We had left Algeria so if we had to come back we would need new visas and that could be complicated.

In 1980 Algeria was going through a relatively safe period in its recent history. Following a turbulent time in the late 1980s, the country began a civil war that lasted from 1991 to 2002. Estimates of civilian deaths during that war vary, but there were many massacres in villages and towns.

9

MOROCCO

WEDDING PARTY

Figuig is an oasis town on the southeastern tip of Morocco, surrounded by Algeria on three sides and dominated by a small range of mountains. Historically this lovely red ochre town played a major role on the routes of the trans-Saharan caravan trade.

There is a long history of conflict between Morocco and Algeria, which started when Algeria was still a colony of France. In the mid 1970s Spain announced it would relinquish control of the region called Western Sahara. Morocco claimed ownership while Algeria supported the independence movement. For many years there was a war of independence and as a result poor relationships between Algeria and Morocco.

This conflict was unresolved in 1980 and as a result Rob and I were not confident we could cross this border. But we did and received a very warm welcome from the Moroccan border guards and customs. Whether we would have received this were we Algerians is another matter. I suspected that the welcome was based on the fact that two Western travellers arriving on foot was unusual and a bit of an event. Mint tea and pastries were brought out and we sat with the small number of officers and enjoyed their hospitality.

It was around 1pm when we left the border post and walked the remaining two and a half miles into the town. We found a small café and ate yet another beautiful meal of couscous and vegetables. We were just finishing up when a soldier appeared in full combat uniform with a rifle over his shoulder. At the start of my journey I

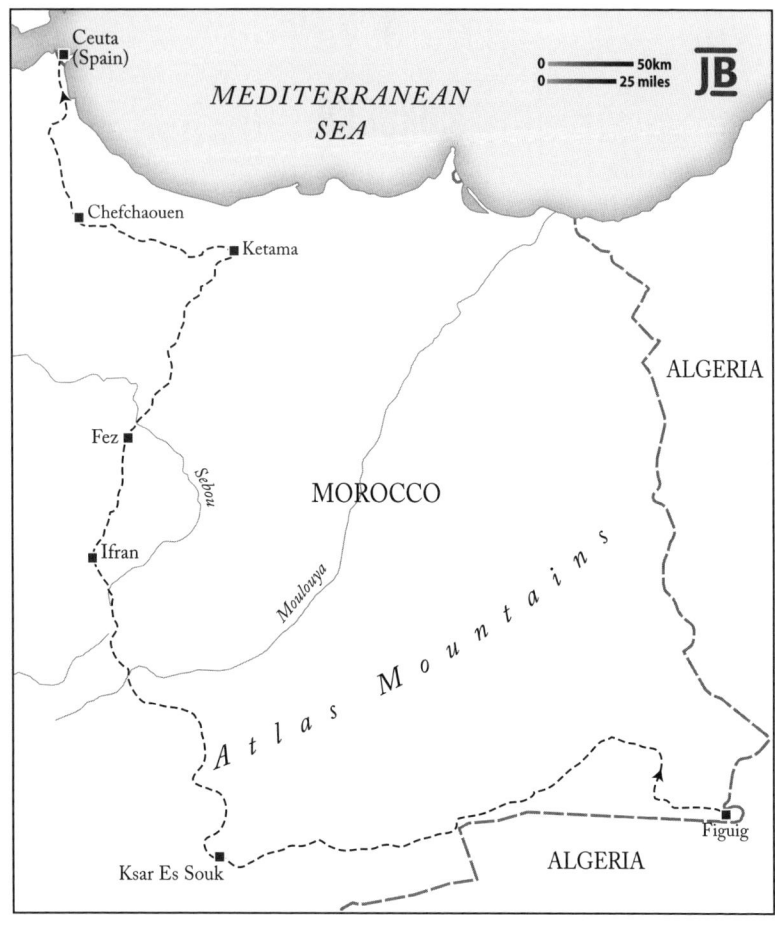

would have found this alarming but I was pretty used to meeting soldiers and police now. He sat down at our table and immediately engaged us in conversation.

'What are you doing here in Figuig?' he asked.

Rob replied, 'We are both towards the end of long journeys across much of North and Central Africa. We have just crossed the border from Algeria.'

'Welcome to Morocco,' he said. 'My name is Ouajdi and I would like to hear about your journeys.'

We were happy to talk and he ordered a round of mint tea and pastries. He was very enthusiastic and excited about our travels. After an hour of intense conversation he invited us to come and stay with him and his wife. We spent the night with them and they were very generous, although they kept giving us presents which of course we could not refuse. The problem was that we had nothing to offer them back, literally nothing apart from one of my dwindling stock of postcards. We had a lovely evening. They were very interested in hearing our stories and were extremely hospitable. I hoped that we sang for our supper.

The next morning we walked to the edge of the town to try and hitch a lift. Quite a few cars passed by but no one stopped. We suspected, given the welcoming arrival we had received, that few Westerners travelled through this remote border area. Maybe drivers were cautious of us and to be honest we both looked pretty rough after months of often hard travelling. Eventually we got a bus to the town of Ksar Es Souk, passing through the desert with mountains in the distance. There was a lot of rain again but thankfully it had stopped before we arrived in the town after dark and somehow found the campsite.

The next morning we went to explore Ksar Es Souk. We found a café and had mint tea and a snack and got into conversation with Ghazil and Haroun, two locals of about my age. They were lovely and spoke perfect French and pretty good English.

'Can you tell us about Paris and London?' asked Ghazil. 'We want to leave here and go to one of these cities. We both have a good education.'

I always found this a difficult question and tried to talk about some of the many sides of London. 'London is a very busy city which has wealth but also a lot of poverty. If you can get a visa that allows you to work and you can get a good job, you should be OK. But it would be a difficult place to live without a good job and there can be prejudice towards people from Africa.'

They wanted to leave the town as there was little or no opportunity for people with education. I didn't want to put them off and could see the challenges they faced staying here. The town was old and very traditional, and all that lay ahead if they stayed was getting married and working in their family businesses, both small shops. It was a dilemma I had met again and again over most of my travels in Africa.

They both had to go off to work in their family shops but as they left they said, 'You must come to the wedding tonight in our village.'

'Are you sure that we would be welcome?' I asked, to which their reply in unison was, 'Of course!'

We arranged to meet them later and as the sun was falling we walked together to their village, which was about 20 minutes from the campsite. The village consisted of 12 red ochre mud houses built around a square. There was a stage set up in the square and already plenty of people. The women were dressed in beautiful traditional *djellabas* with sashes around the waist, mostly red headscarves and ornate necklaces. Most of the men were wearing white *djellabas* and luckily Rob and I were too.

Almost immediately there a horn played on the stage and our friends took each of us to a different house where we sat on the floor on cushions laid out around the sides of the main room.

As soon as the room was full of men seated around the walls, women arrived and served a delicious meal of couscous and vegetables. Meat was offered as well but surprisingly many of the men refused this so I didn't feel awkward. After the meal was over, we were all passed metal goblets and two of the women walked around pouring mint tea into these. We were then offered little brass bowls filled with water to wash our hands.

Over the meal many of the older men asked me what we were doing there. I told them about my journey, which they found extraordinary. They were very surprised to see Western travellers there at all as the border with Algeria had been closed for so long and many thought it still was.

Then we were off outside to the square where by now there was a band of musicians on the stage. A group of seven men played mandolins, a violin, drums and some other percussion, with about five women seated at the side of the stage singing. After a few songs the women started dancing, gyrating so fast that the light on the stage looked like a strobe light. It was a very beautiful sight and soon the whole square was full of everyone dancing, including me and Rob. At some point the bride and groom walked on to the stage and everyone started cheering. The bride was wearing a red patterned *djellaba*, with a huge, colourful necklace, large silver earrings and a white head cover with silver hanging down over her forehead.

I was a bit overwhelmed by the generosity of the villagers inviting us to be part of a wedding. It was hard to imagine this happening at home. It was a really lovely evening and we stayed late until the wedding party started to end, and after saying thank you to literally one hundred people, which took a while, we walked back to the campsite in the dark.

ATLAS MOUNTAINS

We woke a bit later than usual and to our surprise there was a car parked next to us and two women eating their breakfast. We woke to the sound of laughter. 'You have both slept in very late,' they said as they kept laughing.

'We were up until late at a wedding last night and then walked back in the dark,' I explained. 'I think we deserve a lie-in.'

'That's allowed,' said one of them. 'Would you like to share our breakfast? We are Sophie and Lina from Munich.'

'Thank you very much, we'd like that,' said Rob.

We chatted over breakfast with Sophie and Lina. 'Where are you heading next?' asked Lina.

'We're off to Fez,' I said.

'Would you like a lift part of the way?' she asked.

Of course we accepted. They drove us up a winding road that went through the passes of the Haut Atlas, the tall mountain range of Morocco. The mountains were majestic and we drove on through the Middle Atlas which was more wooded. Somewhere we stopped in a small village and found a small café and then carried on. The drive took about five hours, offering views of lush green forest and mountain peaks above. All the while we chatted away, telling tales of our respective travels. Lina and Sophie were driving around Morocco in a car they had driven from Germany and had a few weeks before they had to get back to Munich for university.

Mid-afternoon we drove into Ifran, which was a bit of a shock. It was like an alpine town, with large houses on wide streets, surrounded by trees and large gardens. The houses had tall, peaked, sloping roofs very similar to Swiss mountain houses. There were fountains in the public spaces and a minaret that looked out of place.

There were French-style cafés and clearly it was a resort that got plenty of snow in the winter. After eight months away from home, I had not expected to feel like I was in Europe so soon, although that was the day that I started to feel the pull of home.

We found a campsite and the four of us headed out to eat. Very grateful for the lift, Rob and I bought Sophie and Lina dinner at the cheapest restaurant we could find. They didn't seem to mind that we were such cheapskates and we had a fun evening.

The next morning we said goodbye to our new friends, who were heading to Rabat via Meknes. They offered to take us there but Rob and I were keen to go to Fez as we had heard a lot of great stories about this historical city. And although we hadn't really talked about it much, we were both feeling ready to head home. I was getting low on money and wasn't sure if I would have enough to get back to the UK via Spain and France. And I was still feeling tired. I put this to the back of my mind for now.

We got a lift from a local trader heading to Fez. We sat in the back of his pickup van, bouncing around on the bumpy roads for about two hours, but being outside we were cooled by the breeze as we drove along. Soon we entered the outskirts of the city of Fez.

ANCIENT CITY

Today Fez, founded during the 8th and 9th centuries, is the second-largest city in Morocco. It became a UNESCO World Heritage Site in 1981. The fact about Fez that most got my attention was that its University of al-Qarawiyyin is considered by many to be the oldest continually operating university in the world. It was founded as a mosque in 859CE and was one of the leading spiritual and educational centres in the Muslim world.

All this was waiting for us as our driver dropped us in the modern, French part of the city. Suddenly we were in the midst of boulevards, cafés and shops. We could have been in a town in southern France. We offered our driver a coffee in one of the many cafés but he said he was in a hurry to get to the Medina. We didn't know what that meant at that point, but soon found out.

We walked a little and soon enough the wide boulevards and cafés gave way to narrow streets and colourful stalls selling pretty much everything. Rob suddenly looked rough and said that he felt unwell so I focused on finding us somewhere to stay, which wasn't difficult. The challenge was trying to avoid the hordes of children asking us for money to 'find' a hotel for us. I could see that Rob was in trouble so went into the first door in a wall that looked like it might be a hotel and thankfully it was. Behind the wall was a courtyard with small rooms around the side and we took one of these. There was a communal set of toilets and Rob went off there and didn't come back for a while. He had dysentery. I had had this a few times on the journey so knew that all he would want was a bed, clean water and access to a toilet – in a hurry. I made sure that Rob had enough water and was comfortable in the bed, then left him there and walked back to the modern area, braving the crowds of children, and found a pharmacy where I got Rob some medication. Once I had administered this to the patient and left him to sleep, I headed off to explore the Medina.

I had spent time in the *souks* of Cairo but was unprepared for the sensory experience of this ancient city. Very quickly I felt that I had gone back in time many centuries. I really liked the architecture. There were colourful mosaic water points dotted around and solid wooden doors on the buildings. The streets were narrow, packed with shops, stalls, coffee and *shi* shops, soup kitchens and other food stalls. I would occasionally see someone enter or leave through doors from buildings in the walls of the tiny streets. I'd have loved to have gone through one of these doors, but obviously didn't. The streets were way too narrow for vehicles so everything was carried around on hand-drawn carts or the backs of donkeys. There were fabrics of every possible colour hanging out at the front of stalls that were crammed inside. The smells were overwhelming, smells of spices, smoke, cooked food and excrement from the donkeys and other animals. There were old mosques, beautiful gates and blue and white tiles on many of the walls. And people everywhere. I'd never seen streets so busy. 'Welcome my friend,' was said a lot and it was hard to avoid being corralled into taking a tour with one of the many 'tour guides'. I must have wandered for hours and lost all sense of time until darkness fell. I found somewhere to eat couscous and vegetables before winding my way back to the hotel. It took a while and a few false turns to find it again and it was dark when I arrived. Rob was fast asleep and I quietly crawled into the other bed.

The next day Rob was still ill so I got him fresh water and a piece of dry bread. I then wandered the old Medina again, and stumbled across the famous Chouara Tannery. On this occasion I paid some money to Ammar, one of the local 'guides' who told me all about how the tannery worked. It was made up of numerous stone vats filled with different coloured dyes and white liquids. Hides of cows, sheep, goats and camels were processed by first soaking them in a series of white liquids made from various mixtures of cow urine, pigeon faeces, quicklime, salt and water to soften the tough skins. This process would take a few days after which the hides were soaked in the dyeing solutions, using natural colours such as indigo, turmeric, poppy and henna. Once dyed, the hides dried under the sun and then the leather was sold to craftsmen, most of whom worked in the Medina. I was fascinated by this process, all done by hand in the same way as in medieval times.

I liked Ammar, who was keen to be my guide for the rest of the day. To be honest, despite the small amount of money I had left, it was a lot more fun and interesting to see the city with him. After we left the tannery, he took me to a barber as my hair was a mess. I hated visiting the barber as a child, but this was the best haircut I had ever had. The barber was gentle and slow and kept holding up a mirror for me to see progress. At the end he gave me a shave and I left feeling fantastic. After that we had a bite to eat in a café before heading off into parts of the *souk* that I suspect I would not have otherwise found. With Ammar it was easy to go into a shop to look around without getting stuck in a lengthy price negotiation for something I didn't really want. Browsing was not really an option without local help. We spent the afternoon looking at stalls selling clothes, rugs, silver and gold jewellery, spices, books, herbal remedies and other medicines. As I was nearly at the end of my trip I thought that I could afford a few small gifts for the family and I had my eye on a rug that I had seen in one of the stalls.

I had learned a little of the noble art of bargaining in Jerusalem and Cairo early on in my journey, but the shop owners and traders of Fez were at a whole other level of skill. I guess that was partly as the city was quite a popular tourist destination, although it was long before the days of cheap flights. Ammar was very helpful and explained that if after twenty minutes the bargaining had still not resulted in an acceptable price for my budget, I should thank the shopkeeper, walk out and head up the street. The shopkeeper would almost certainly come running up after me with an improved offer.

The next day Rob felt much better and I bought him some simple food to eat in the room. It wasn't much but he managed to hold it down and then decided he wanted to walk around the *souk* a bit. We set off and soon Ammar appeared and we negotiated a small rate for the day. Rob enjoyed it although he needed to go back to lie down after a couple of hours. I went back with him, and then Ammar and I set off again. He wanted to introduce me to his friend Salah so we met him in a small café for mint tea and then went to his small shop and smoked some hashish, which Morocco was famous for. I spent much of the rest of the day hanging out with Salah and Ammar and we talked a lot about what we wanted to do with our lives.

The days rolled past. Rob was feeling better but still quite weak and it didn't seem right to move on until he was ready. He was enjoying his time walking in the *souk* but by now I was feeling ready to head back home. I felt like the Africa journey was ending. I enjoyed Fez but felt like a tourist rather than the traveller I had become. My mood was low, and I was starting to feel homesick. But I also felt trepidation about what I would do with my life and the pressures that I would feel to start some form of career. I realised that this journey had been partly a means of avoiding this. I had conflicted feelings and an overwhelming sense of many things coming to an end – the journey, my time with Rob, and the freedom I had felt this year.

I bought a few small gifts for my sisters. But I wanted something for myself that would remind me of this journey. I had seen a blanket that I really liked a couple of days earlier. It was brown and white in the style made by the Berbers, the original indigenous people of North Africa. The Tuaregs, whom I had met in the Sahara, are a Berber ethnic group.

Ammar and I went to the stall where this blanket was on sale and then began a four-hour haggle. It started with a casual look around the shop, where I ignored the blanket that I really wanted. The shopkeeper then started showing me rugs and blankets that he thought I would like. I was nonchalant, but I took an interest in a couple of them. Mint tea was brought, along with pastries, and we sat while he explained how valuable and well made his products were. When he finally shared a price, which was quite high, I said no, I did not think I wanted one of those. Eventually he showed me the blanket that I wanted. We had been in the shop for two hours by now.

At this point the haggle went to another level. More tea was brought. The initial price was high, more than I could afford, but less than the price of the previous two. I said 'too much', and after much discussion about the provenance of the blanket a price of about 60% of where he had started was on the table. 'Thank you so much for your kind offer,' I said, 'but I still cannot afford your price.'

'What is your best price?' he asked. I gave him a price that was about 20% of where he had started. Now we were bargaining. This went on for another half-hour or so and we were at about 50%. It was probably a reasonably fair price, but I was running short of money and unless I got work on my way home I would struggle to get across Europe. We hit an impasse.

Ammar quietly said, 'Let's get up and leave.' We left, saying '*shkran*' many times, and with much shaking of hands we walked slowly out of the shop and up the passage outside. Sure enough the shopkeeper quickly followed us and offered a lower price. Ammar and I looked at each other and with some shaking of heads finally agreed to go back. Eventually I got the blanket for just about 30% of where we had started and Ammar agreed that this was a fair price. Now it was all smiles and shaking of hands and more tea and pastries while the money was counted out and handed over. I still have the blanket today.

By now we had been six days in Fez. Rob was much better and ready to head back to Europe. But he had one thing he wanted to do: visit Ketama, the region where most of Morocco's cannabis was grown. I wasn't at all sure about this and considered whether it was time to leave Rob to his own devices.

CANNABIS

I had introduced Rob to Ammar's friend Salah and they started talking about going to Salah's home in Ketama town to try some of the best cannabis. Again, I wasn't sure about this, but in the end I went with them. We travelled in his friend's car so four of us were crammed in. It was a drive up into the hills above Fez and once we left the city, joints started being passed around.

We arrived at Ketama in the middle of the afternoon and I was worse for wear. We were introduced to Salah's family who were lovely and had made up a small room for Rob and me. We drank some tea and ate some food and then went for a walk around the town, eventually ending up at a friend's house where more hashish was smoked.

It seemed like the whole town was smoking hashish and I asked Salah about this. 'Ketama is different to the rest of Morocco,' he said.

'This is the area where most of the cannabis is grown and processed into the blocks of hash for illegal export. The government turns a blind eye to the production of cannabis resin because it provides livelihoods for pretty much everyone in the region.'

I wasn't sure about this at the time but when I was preparing to write this book, I came across a 2017 report published by the non-sectarian research and advocacy Transnational Institute called 'Morocco and Cannabis: Reduction, containment or acceptance'[22] and was struck by two of the key points:

The unregulated cannabis market in Morocco has negative social consequences. Some 48,000 growers have arrest warrants hanging over their heads, which is a source of corruption and repression. An amnesty and decriminalisation could be effective measures to diminish negative social consequences and open the debate about regulation.

Cannabis farmers in Morocco should have access to emerging legally regulated cannabis markets that are gaining ground worldwide. The challenge is to find a sustainable development model that includes cannabis cultivation in Morocco, instead of excluding cannabis and ignoring the realities of more than 50 years of failed attempts to eradicate the only viable economic option in the region.

That evening we were invited to a wedding. Like the wedding in Ksar Es Souk, the whole village was present for the celebration. The women were dressed in colourful clothing. There was much blowing of horns and beating of drums and the women were dancing while

---

22   tni.org/files/publication-downloads/dpb_49_eng_web.pdf

most of the men hung around the edges of the wedding in small groups. It was the women who appeared to keep the culture alive. A lot of the younger men were 'cool guys' with clothes to match, mostly European hand-me-downs. There were a lot of 'F**k you's spoken in American English with a Moroccan accent, which sounded really funny.

The next day we left Salah and his friends in Ketama. Like so many people Salah and his friends and family had been very generous but I was glad to leave them as I found the endless smoking of hashish tedious. Also as we got closer to Europe my feeling that I was ready to go back home got stronger, although I wasn't sure why. I had no job, no partner, no home (other than with my parents) and really no idea what I wanted to do next with my life. I wondered whether I might get some work for a while, save up and head off to India, which I'd always wanted to do. But I didn't think too much about all that. Since leaving Fez I had felt a strange pull to get back to London and I followed it.

I had spent more than expected in Fez and was very nearly out of money. I'd set off with £250 and to my amazement it had almost been enough. Travelling with Rob had really helped me reduce my travel costs, as we had rarely paid for travel or places to stay and had often been given meals for free. The generosity of people was extraordinary, and I only hoped that the time I had spent in so many communities along the route was something that they had enjoyed too. I tried not to feel guilty for being a white man coming from one of the wealthiest countries in the world arriving at villages looking for somewhere to stay. I had spent time in four of the five poorest countries in the world and yet in all of these I had been welcomed into people's homes and in more than one case taken care of when I was ill.

As we had done so many times we started walking out of town, this time surrounded by small boys trying to sell us hashish. Eventually a car stopped and we got in with two older Moroccan men. They didn't speak much French but we managed to tell them something of our travels, which they seemed very interested in. They stopped at the small town of Bab Taza after about two and a half hours of winding roads and hairpin bends in the absolutely beautiful, wooded mountains of northern Morocco.

We found a small café, had a bite to eat and decided to see if we could get a ride to Chefchaouen by the end of the day. As we left the town the rain started falling and pretty soon we were absolutely drenched. Luckily another car stopped for us which was really kind as we soaked the back seats of his car. This time Arij the driver spoke French so we could chat most of the way, mainly answering his questions about the many countries we had travelled through. The rain stopped in time for us to arrive in Chefchaouen in glorious sunshine.

LAST DAY

Chefchaouen is a beautiful town nestled up against the mountains. The houses are almost all blue and white, a bit like on many of the Greek islands. The streets were narrow with steep stairs, lined with houses, small shops, cafés, restaurants and mosques.

We found a small hotel where they let us sleep on the roof for very little, and we prayed that the rain would not return. It didn't. It was a lot less expensive than Fez, and people were very relaxed. We didn't have anyone trying to sell us anything. It was lovely.

From the late 1400s, Chefchaouen served as a Moorish fortress for Spanish exiles, welcoming Jews and Christians. Jewish teachings suggested that by dyeing thread with *tekhelel*, an ancient natural dye and weaving it into prayer shawls, people would be reminded of God's power. This is one explanation for the preponderance of blue buildings in the town, as in some way the colour blue represents the divine.

We had both decided to leave the next day to head to Spain and from there back to the UK. So this would be our last full day in Africa – and it was a beautiful one. The sun was shining and the blue buildings were mesmerising in the sunlight. We walked around the streets of the town, sitting in cafés with a mint tea when we got tired. I wished I had a bit more money to buy some gifts but that wasn't an option. In the evening we ate a stunning vegetable tagine, the traditional Moroccan dish of vegetables, spices and oil served on a bed of fluffy couscous. We lay out on the roof of the hotel looking at the sky full of stars. It was a perfect end to my last day in Africa.

10

EUROPE

VENDANGES

With mixed emotions we set off from Chefchaouen to travel the 65 miles to the border between Morocco and Spain at Ceuta: sadness at leaving Africa but also excitement at finally heading back home. We got a lift to the city of Tetouan where after some enquiries we discovered that the only realistic way to get to Ceuta was on the bus. We could get a lift in a car but the majority were pulled apart by the Spanish customs looking for drugs and it could take a long time to get through. It would be worse if the driver was found carrying drugs, involving a significant risk on our part. It was early afternoon when we arrived at the border.

Ceuta is a strange colonial oddity, much like Gibraltar. It became part of Spain in 1668. When Morocco gained independence in 1956, Spain considered Ceuta an integral part of the Spanish state, but Morocco has disputed this ever since in much the same way that Spain disputes the British ownership of Gibraltar. We crossed the border quickly and easily along with the other passengers on the bus and headed to the ferry port. To my great relief I had enough money left to pay for the ferry and a few days of cheap food. I had to hope that I could get work picking grapes in France.

Rob and I had decided that we would go our separate ways again once we reached Algeciras. He wanted to get home and unlike me had not completely run out of money. We sat together in silence on the deck of the ferry between Ceuta and Algeciras in Spain. I was tearful watching the continent of Africa slowly disappear into the mist. We arrived at the port of Algeciras and Rob and I said goodbye. Two endings at once.

I stopped at a bar in Algeciras and despite my limited funds had a small glass of beer. I suddenly felt I needed this. Other than the few local brews I'd been offered, this was the first beer I'd had for the whole year. I set off walking out of the town, turning around every few minutes and holding my hand out for a lift. Many cars passed, more than had passed me on any other day in the last nine months.

It got dark and I found a van on the side of the road cooking pizzas. There were a few young people there and I decided to spend some of my last cash on a pizza. While I was waiting I asked some of the Spaniards whether there was somewhere I could sleep outside safely. They were lovely and two of them took me to a small park nearby where I slept well hidden under a large bush.

I woke early under my bush feeling stiff with a raging headache and smelling pretty bad. I found a public toilet and had a wash at the sink. There was a mirror and I saw myself for the first time in months. I looked terrible. I was really thin, my skin was blotchy and my hair was matted. My teeth needed a really good clean. I walked back to the road and started hitchhiking again. Again, I was not very successful. I did get a few short lifts from local people which was lovely and they were very kind. One of them bought me lunch, probably taking pity on the smelly, scruffy and skinny young man I had become. It took me the whole day to travel the 86 miles from Algeciras to Malaga by which time it was dark again. I was not taken with the Costa del Sol with its blocks of hotels and apartments, discos, supermarkets and English pubs dotted along the coast road. Just as well that none of these appealed to me as I was really very short of money now.

That evening I did something I had done previously when hitchhiking to Greece. In the distance I could see a road sign marking the end of the town. I walked the few hundred yards to the sign with my hand out, all the while telling myself that if I didn't get a lift by then I would find somewhere to sleep outside. And just as I got to the sign a car stopped.

I opened the door and started speaking in my monosyllabic Spanish and the driver introduced himself in French. What a relief. 'I'm driving to Toulouse overnight and I would welcome the company,' he said.

'Thank you so much,' I replied. 'I've been travelling in Africa for months and have run out of money. I'm heading to the south of France to try to get work in the Vendanges.'

Antoine the driver knew exactly what I meant. The Vendanges is the annual grape harvest in France and attracts lots of young people from across Europe for casual work.

Antoine drove until 11.30pm and stopped at a bar. He bought us each a glass of red wine and we both slept in the car for a few hours. Antoine woke me around 4am and drove off. It was a long day as he drove up through Spain. He wisely stopped quite a few times and had a sleep and sometimes a meal. He was really interested in my travels and I spent many hours telling him in some detail about my journey. He kept asking me questions and as he spoke a bit of English we managed to communicate well. At that point, he probably knew more about my travels than anyone else. We crossed the border into France around midnight but it was clear that Antoine was tired. He had hoped to get home to Toulouse that night, but we found an open bar, had another glass of wine and slept in the car.

We woke after a few hours. Antoine suggested that he drop me near Narbonne and that I make my way to Lézignan-Corbières. He said he was in a hurry now, otherwise he would have taken me himself. I was so grateful for his generosity and said goodbye by the side of the road. I immediately got a lift with a man probably in his mid-50s. He picked me up and I explained that I was heading to Lézignan-Corbières. Yes, that was no problem, he was heading that way.

Except that he didn't. It took me a while to figure out that we were heading in a different direction. I asked him to stop and let me out, but he was silent and drove on faster. Then he reached over and touched my upper leg. I screamed at him and shouted, 'Leave me alone.' I was lucky. I think I shocked him as he stopped the car at the side of the road. I opened the door, grabbed my bag and jumped out. He drove off. I was shaking. I had just hitchhiked thousands of miles in some of the supposedly most dangerous countries in the world and never had experienced anything like this.

By now it was around 10am, I was hungry and it was my 23rd birthday. I had five francs (worth 50 pence) which I had changed at the border and that was all. I walked along the road and came to a small village. I asked for directions to Lézignan-Corbières and to my surprise I was offered a lift there by a local lorry driver who was heading that way. He correctly guessed that I was hungry, offering me half of the baguette and cheese that he had in the cab. I was so grateful. We arrived in Lézignan-Corbières by late morning and I walked around the town until I came to a building surrounded by a small crowd of young people, many of them British. I joined them and discovered that this was the town hall where everyone came to find work in the Vendanges.

I went and registered, speaking in my best French, and was told that my level of fluency would be an advantage but that I was too late for that day. The winemakers came in the morning and they suggested that I come back around 8am the next day. I went back outside and joined a group of Brits, mostly around my age. They wanted to know where I had come from and I explained that I was at the end of a long journey travelling across much of North and Central Africa. A few of us headed to a café nearby and I spent my last five francs on a cheese baguette and a glass of red wine. When they discovered it was my birthday, I was bought a couple more drinks. I asked them where they were staying. 'We slept in a field at the edge of the town,' said one of them. So I slept the night in this field celebrating my 23rd birthday with a group of people I had only just met. We drank wine that a few of them bought from a local shop which warmed me up. Just as well, as this was a cold night for sleeping outside.

The next day we were all back at the temporary Vendanges office in the town and sure enough winemakers started to arrive. My name was called and I met a local farmer who immediately asked me how good my French was. I started speaking to him in French and in no time he said, 'You will do. Find five other people.' I went outside to the four I had spent the night with saying, 'I have got work for us and one other.' They immediately found another and in no time we all had work.

I picked grapes for nearly three weeks. I was earning reasonably good money and now had more than enough to get home. I enjoyed the work and my colleagues. The winemaker, Monsieur Canet, and I spoke French together and I translated between him and the team of British workers. He had a house in his village that we lived in, crowded but lots of fun. It was great to speak English again and I was a bit proud of my role as the translator. The high point was when Monsieur Canet said, 'Patrick, you speak very good French but you sound like an African.'

HOME

After nearly three weeks I was becoming concerned about how tired I was feeling and decided that it was time to head home. I told Monsieur Canet, who was disappointed. I told my co-workers that I was leaving and that they would need to start speaking more French. I left the next day and found it surprisingly easy to get three lifts all the way to Paris. I stopped the night near Clermont-Ferrand, sleeping under a bush. Despite being October it was quite warm. The next morning I got a lift all the way to Paris. I arrived mid-afternoon and made my way straight to the Gare du Nord where I bought a ticket for the night train and ferry that evening. I took the train to Dunkirk, boarded the ferry and then got the train at Dover. It took the whole night and the sun was rising as the train drew into Victoria Station. I found a currency exchange shop at the station, changed my francs into pounds and called my parents' home from a phone box. No one answered.

I arrived at the family home in South London and knocked on the door. There was no reply. I was about to go and find the hidden key when my sister Polly appeared. She was in bed, unwell. I had my first bath in a very long time. My parents were away overseas on a work trip so I settled in. A couple of days and lots of sleep later, I got an appointment at the Tropical Medicine Hospital at St Pancras. I discussed my malaria and other health problems I had had on the journey. The doctor said that I would probably experience malaria symptoms for the rest of my life, which wasn't very encouraging. I explained that I was feeling unusually tired and his response was that under the circumstances of my travels, he wasn't surprised. He told me to get some rest.

I went home and did just that. Three days later I went to the bathroom and saw that my urine was dark. I looked in the mirror and my face looked jaundiced. It had to be hepatitis A. I called the Tropical Medicine Hospital and they sent an ambulance to get me, with the staff wearing protective clothing and masks. I was whisked to the hospital and spent the next 10 days in an isolation ward. I was given medicine, injections and food by nurses in protective clothing. By now my parents had returned and my dad came to visit me every evening, also in protective clothing. Those days were a blur. I slept a lot and ate very little, avoiding fatty foods. I drank a lot of water. It would be many years before I drank any alcohol as it's vital to protect the liver after hepatitis.

When I came out of hospital I had a week's recovery at my parents' house. I woke up one morning realising I needed to do something. So I went down to the local job centre and looked for work. As I looked at the cards on the boards my eyes blurred and I couldn't really read them. And then I had this thought:

'Go back to Bristol and set up a wholefoods wholesale company.'

Where did that come from? I stood gazing at the job cards but not reading them. Then I remembered the conversation with Rob in Juba.

I still knew a few people in Bristol, made some calls and was offered somewhere to stay for a short time by a friend. I packed a bag, got the bus to Hammersmith and hitchhiked down.

And the rest of my life began.

LOOSE ENDS

Before I went back to Bristol, I sought out the Singer shop in Covent Garden. I showed them the handwritten notes I had on the Singer parts and to my great surprise they had them in stock. I bought six of everything, packed them up into two packages and went around to a nearby post office. It cost a lot of money to post them to Goma, but I did it. I enclosed a letter to Gildas and Alain and their father with my parents' address, asking them to reply to tell me they had received the parts. I never heard back and can only hope that at least one of the packages arrived.

Over the next few years I wrote many times to Michael who took me in when I had malaria in Central African Republic but have never heard anything from him. I try not to worry about this.

Rob made contact after I got out of hospital and we met up. We were both at a loose end but agreed to stay in touch. Just a few days later I started what became my career as a social entrepreneur. Nine months later Rob came to work with us at Nova Wholefoods in Bristol but after a year or so he left. We lost contact after that.

After I moved to Bristol, I kept getting bouts of fever every six weeks. I went to a GP who said it was the recurrent malaria and that I would need to get used to it. I wasn't happy and my business partner suggested I visit a local herbalist. He listened to my story of malaria and made up two herbal liquid concoctions for me to drink over the next month. I have not had the malaria fever since, although I do have a tendency to have headaches. I became a fan of herbal medicines.

If you are interested in what happened to me next, I had an unconventional but successful career as a social entrepreneur, starting up, growing and leading 12 businesses, charities and co-operatives. You can read all about my 40 years as a social entrepreneur in my book *Creating Social Enterprise: My story and what I learned*, available on Amazon.

I have been back to Morocco three times and Egypt once. Other than that I've not returned to Africa. I never made it to Swaziland (now called Eswatini) but my youngest daughter went to an international sixth form college there for two years. So at least one of us made it there!

For those of you who like data, here are the figures: I travelled 14,359 miles overland from Tel Aviv to London, of which 12,642 miles were in Africa. The journey took me through Israel, Gaza (not technically a country yet), Egypt, Sudan, South Sudan (a new country after 2011), Uganda, Kenya, Zaire (now Democratic Republic of Congo), Central African Republic, Cameroon, Nigeria, Niger, Algeria, Morocco, Spain and France. The vast majority of this was on foot, on lorries and in shared 'taxis'. I took four train journeys and one ferry journey on Lake Aswan, and hitched a ride on a cargo boat on the Congo River.

It was a journey that changed me forever. Little did I know as I returned that I had absorbed an approach to life and values that would mark the rest of my life and career. I am so grateful for the opportunity to travel across so much of the continent of Africa, a journey that would be much harder today.

Thank you for reading my story.